GREET

**CHARACTER THAT INFLUENCES
RELATIONSHIPS**

OYEWOLA OYELEKE

Dedication

To My Mum, your love showed me the reason for living and living rightly. And my late Dad, whose love and sincere parental training taught me common sense, the simple value of good character, conduct and performance.

This is also to my loving wife, so much support to get me to this form.

Published Year 2020
By Home Front Corporations
494 Stuyvesant Avenue
Irvington
07111, NJ, USA
Telephone: +1 201 349 8020
Website: www.homefrontpublications.com
ISBN 978-0-578-23630-8

SUPPORT FOR CHARITY

10% of all author royalties are donated to charity.
Help to Ageing Foundation (HAF),
GreenFaith for World Health and climate change
Books for Schools and ChildFund.

TABLE OF CONTENTS

Acknowledgement

My appreciation goes to my life coach and pastor, Dr. Chris Oyakhilome PhD, DD., who has been the mouthpiece of God to me.

I also want to thank my wife, Nkechi, the woman with a great heart, always standing by me through dark and thin, she is just an angel.

A special thank you to my teachers, who inspired me from start to finish,

Archbishop +Mark Anthony, GOC. Metropolitan of Lagos and Exarch of West Africa.

The most Reverend (Archbishop) Dr. Joseph Alexander, Presiding prelate, New Covenant Christian Ministry.

Not forgetting Tubosun Olaloku, Tosin Kolawole and Lynda O'Neal. Your sacrificial love and support with words and action is appreciated.

Thanks to my beta readers who helped me scout for errors, Ola Aboderin, Smart Sunday Badejo.

And most of all, I thank my readers, all of you. My work will not be a success without your patronage and commitment to reading and recommending this book to many others.

INTRODUCTION

WHO WE ARE

The subject of courtesy (and greeting, in particular) is an unusual theme of discussion - especially in this post-modern era in which human interaction is not only being minimized but trivialized. Yet, it is one that is profoundly significant for a peaceful and successful life. To start with, greeting goes beyond merely saying a quick "Hi", "Hello" or "Good morning" to someone. It is a way of life on its own. It is an expression of etiquette, which has the power to improve our relationship with others, maximize our impact on people's lives and ultimately create a good life for us.

Our manners broadcast our nature and can chart the path of our destiny. This means that, if not responsibly managed, our manners could deprive us of vital opportunities and advantages in life. This is exactly why we are exploring this subject, so we can learn the way to live the good life by doing the right things and in the right way.

The saying is indeed true that it is the child who opens wide his arms that gets lifted and embraced by an older person. We can get attention and favors from the least expected places and people because of some rare but endearing virtues we possess. Indeed, a major paradox of life is that it is those character traits that many people are not mindful of that make the difference in our lives and hold the key to our success. Such attributes could be as simple as a greeting, a soothing word, or a kind gesture – and yet they could make all the difference.

It is what we do right that makes others around us to feel happy and inspired. And isn't this the greatest pursuit of life – to brighten the lives of others, while seeking to fulfil our own purpose? Yet, there are many who ignore this crucial opportunity because they think it is not everybody who deserves their respect or because they simply do not think it has anything to do with their ultimate fulfilment.

Every man's success is not in the amount of money they have stacked up in the bank or the numerous properties they have acquired, but the lives they have touched and the lives they have impacted into brightness and happiness, the life that is reformed and encouraged to be the best without expecting a return, you can easily judge the character of a man by how he treats those who can do nothing for him.

We make the world a better place for ourselves and everyone else when we reflect a courteous attitude towards those, we share space with and to those that seem less important to us. When we greet and treat them with respect, we make them feel good about themselves. On our own side, too, we can gain the attention of those who ordinarily, would have preferred to ignore us. Our good manners pave the way for us to receive their heartfelt permission to "enter the vaults and carry the gold" – a proof that we are often the ultimate beneficiaries with those whose hearts we manage to win. The secret to making this conquest and reaping the rewards is one of the key revelations in this book.

It will definitely interest you to know that this

book is the result of over three years of intense research and interviews with individuals and groups from different backgrounds who have been affected by the impact of this most ignored activity, **greeting.** I took time to study people's questions and comments; and I also analyzed the reports of individuals and professionals who have had one experience or two with other people in this area – people they greeted and those they did not greet; people that greeted them and those they were expecting a greeting from but did not greet them – as well as the responses they got by the greetings they made and the relationships some were able to form.

I also had extensive discussions with people who had been affected one way or the other in their marriages and other relationships by the power of courtesy and greeting. Many of these people revealed that their marriages were saved by showing such basic manners as greeting. Others admitted that it created avenues for them to mend their broken relationships, while a few more told me that it opened incredible opportunities for them with people who were known to be difficult and sarcastic.

Let me assure you that, while it may take you some hours to explore the contents of this book, the depths of insights and inspirations you will receive will certainly last you a lifetime, I recommend that you don't rush through this book, read it with rapt attention. Refuse to read it as you would read a journal or novel or the commonplace inspirational book, it should be as a work of enlightenment which is meant to unravel the hidden, inner qualities of a soul in search of self-discovery, and a pathway to genuine success in life. The question is: Do you have regular problems and misunderstandings with your spouse, friends, and colleagues? Are you having a hard time with your employer? You certainly can turn things around in your favor by finding your way into this new lifestyle of meekness and responsibility. Start to **greet**!

1
WHAT IS IN A GREETING?
"One *hello* can change a life. One *hello* can save a life."
- Liza M. Wiemer

As soon as Noor Tasnim of Global Health Institute (Duke University) stepped on the dock of Santa Cruz La Laguna, in Guatemala, he knew that the town's residents could easily tell that he was a stranger. There was a lot to give him away – his physical appearance, his backpack, his new pair of Chacos and a few other hints. Yet, he and his team were expected to stay in the region for eight weeks to carry out their research mission.

Noor began to wonder if he would ever fit in. A flurry of worries flooded his mind: How could he make the foreign town his new home in such a short amount of time? Would he ever feel connected to the communities that his team was supposed to work with? Would they ever make a success of this mission? Panicky, he put a call through to the team's advisor to share his concerns. The advisor, who was apparently very experienced, gave what he described as a fail-proof strategy - to greet every stranger they walked by!

From that moment onwards, Noor and his teammates decided to put the advice into practice. They smiled and sang *"Buenos Dias!"* (Good morning) to all the adults and children they passed on their way to their research site in the morning. As they did and got positive feedbacks from the locals, they got so carried away with excitement that even when it was already afternoon, they were still singing *"Buenos Dias"*, until they checked their watches, and realized that they should have been saying *"Buena tardes!"* instead. Fortunately, the townies understood and indulged them. Finally, as the sun prepared to set, they greeted the people they came across with *"Buena noches!"*, as they returned home to reflect on their day's work.

Now, this is the most interesting part. Throughout the duration of the team's assignment – which turned out to be a huge success - the effect of that decision to happily greet the townies proved to be magical. As Noor himself later testified, "Little did I know that such a common greeting could be so powerful. By acknowledging others in the community and having that acknowledgement reciprocated, I felt connected to the indigenous Maya people in the Lake Atitlán region of Guatemala. Within the first week of my trip, the feeling of being an outsider vanished, and I felt accepted by the communities that my team interacted with. It is amazing how a simple nod and smile can considerably increase one's sense of connection to the people around them."

Universal Application
You could call the above illustration a holistic picture of the power of good manners, in general, and greeting, in particular. The breakthrough and success recorded by Noor and his team came through their ability to put one of the most neglected tonics of interpersonal relationships into good use. The more interesting truth however is that such

success can occur in any other settings, using the same approach. In fact, much of the brick wall and breakdown that many people experience in their lives and relationship is because they have not understood this simple secret.

Take marriage, for example, it may not be common to hear a marriage counselor advise a couple that the cause of their marital problem is inability to greet properly. Yet, the truth remains that if a couple can lovingly, sincerely and attentively greet each other every day, saying nice words of affirmation and thoughtfulness, it will not only strengthen the bond between them but will also awaken a deeper sense of responsibility towards each other. This way, many flaws and offenses can be overlooked.

You may consider this assertion about the potential impact of greeting in a couple's relationship to be exaggerated, until you get a good understanding of what greeting actually is. Greeting goes beyond the routine "Good morning", "Good afternoon", "Good evening" and so on – which, by the way, are powerful expressions in themselves, as we shall be seeing shortly; it involves so much more that will definitely interest you to know. The dictionary defines "greeting" as "a polite word or sign of welcome or recognition"; or "an expression of goodwill, said on meeting or in a written message". Indeed, according to the Wikipedia, "A greeting can consist of an exchange of formal expression, kisses, handshakes, hugs, and various gestures."

We recognize then that greetings involve politeness, respect, humility, recognition of the other person, as well as an expression of good wishes upon others. Now, you can see why this should be effective in a marriage, just like in every other relationship. If a man can acknowledge the beauty, virtues, and efforts of his wife often – sincerely saying it with the spoken or written word – she will be happy with him most of the time. The same happens the other way round. If a woman can affirm the worth and contributions of her husband through her greetings, he will certainly feel respected and appreciated, which will go a long way in fostering peace and harmony in the home. Bestselling author, Gretchen Rubin, was a beneficiary of this and she counsels, "Give warm greetings and farewells. I was surprised by how much this resolution changed the atmosphere of my home."

It is the same effect that greetings, done from the bottom of the heart, has on virtually every other person. It communicates love, respect, and recognition to them, and they become naturally favorably disposed towards us. Interestingly, even the Almighty God acknowledges and encourages the potency of greetings. Psalm 100:4 makes it clear that access to God's throne is obtained only after acknowledging His goodness and greatness – through thanksgiving and praise. This is why most men of God encourage their congregations to give time to praising God before making any other request. This is because the prayer of praise and thanksgiving is the highest form of prayer; and the best way to reach into God's heart and get whatever we desire is to acknowledge His omnipotence.

Bigger Picture
What we have seen so far is that greeting is a powerful way of portraying our politeness to

others. "First impression," they say, "lasts the longest." As you greet people heartily from day to day, you will give the impression of yourself as a humble, respectful, and delightsome person to be with.

More importantly, however, you should understand that greetings are, often, expressions of good wishes for someone. In other words, when you greet, you are not only showing respect to the individual but also showing that you earnestly desire their wellbeing. As Frank Santoro rightly said, "Good morning! Good afternoon! Good night! These are not just mere greetings. They are powerful blessings, setting the best vibration for the day. Hence, whether it is morning, afternoon, or night, make sure that you say your greeting right!" To know what is right and not do it is the worst cowardice, and that breaks the ego.

On your own part also, greeting helps you to gain attention, no matter how awkward things may initially seem to be for you in an environment or situation. In fact, just as the opening story shows, you gain honor immediately you can sincerely show courtesy to others, and you also position yourself for a beneficial connection and possible breakthrough. Even if it is just a simple "Hi" that you can manage to sincerely say to someone, it can open doors that money can't break in, while also giving you the keys to master your environment and positively impact the lives of others.

And you really do not have to wait for others to take the initiative of greeting before doing the right thing. Just go head and greet. It distinguishes you and shows how refined and mature you really are. Indeed, a sure way to detect people who are narrow-minded and arrogant is to observe how they treat others. There are people who will never take the initiative to greet; instead, they will keep a record of the names of those who did not greet them first. They know the people that have good manners and those who do not. This is why I said that knowing a man's worth does not start with his resume or the amount of wealth and properties he has accumulated, but by the kind of words that proceed out of his mouth and the mindset he carries and portrays to the world. In other words, the easiest way to measure a man's personality is to observe the way he honors and respects others around him.

Marvin Balaye, the keynote speaker at the 2012 Universal Wealth and Mental Health seminar in Delaware, Unites States, said something quite instructive about greeting. He said greeting is a tool with which we assure others, ease their doubts about who we are and define what our intentions are with them. "Your greeting announces your willingness to offer kindness and good wishes to them and this, in turn, makes them confident and trusting," he said.

Associate, not Isolate

People who do not love to greet are usually those who love to be socially and emotionally isolated from the people around them. However, this isolation comes with a huge price – missing out on the many benefits that come with friendly association with others. Prolific writer, Laurie Futterman, said it well, "When you don't greet someone in your day-to-day interactions, you miss out on a human connection. You miss out on the opportunity to learn something about someone. You miss out on an exchange in energy that occurs when two or more humans come together." But then, you need to understand that isolation does not just start or end without escalating. Isolation begins when you make up your mind not to relate with anyone, except they make the first move – and even at that, you still choose to distance yourself as much as possible. You choose not to greet or get acquainted. You basically avoid opportunities and encounters that can bring you closer to those who are supposed to be your friends, who you can share feelings and perspectives with. Gradually, you begin to get a dose of your own medicine as people observe that you would prefer to be left alone, and they leave you alone.

By and by, you really do begin to feel so alone and – worse still – rejected. Since you have spurned all chances of connectivity, it becomes difficult to get in the train of quality human relationships and interactions, even when you need it so badly. The feeling of rejection can be so painful and tormenting. It can impair many aspects of one's life and cause limited progress or even setbacks. Yet, as we have already seen, we are the ones who often bring rejections upon ourselves by ignoring to do what is right at the right time. Rejection from people we are supposed to lean on or go to when the road becomes tough on us, those we would have ordinarily called upon when we need an arm to lay our head on, If you create isolation, you create a habit. If you create a habit, you create a character. If you create a character, you create a destiny, and such destiny can be that which you finally settle to as a dead end.

Noor Tasnim, whose experience with the Maya people of Guatemala I cited at the beginning of this chapter, gives a deep insight on how to avoid rejection and tap into the power of greetings for ourselves and others. He says: *Many of us experience some sort of rejection on a day-to-day basis. We often may feel ignored or excluded. Although some of us have become desensitized to this feeling, it can still put a damper on anyone's day. However, a greeting can alleviate this sense of rejection. This sort of acknowledgement can make anyone feel more accepted by the people around them and easily brighten their day.*

Of course, the power of greeting made me feel welcomed by the Maya people in Guatemala.

Unfortunately, these interactions contrast experiences we may have with strangers in the various communities. Most of us are sucked into our phones, checking our email, scrolling through Facebook/Instagram, or updating our Snapchat stories. We rarely acknowledge those around us, unless they are someone we know. We can change that. We should try to interact with the people around us. Little may we know that a simple hello/smile can make a huge impact on their day.

Burden of Ignorance

There are people who ignorantly despise the power of greeting by assuming that it is simply a desperate attempt to beg for attention or that greeting is only for those who deserve it. But greeting goes beyond this. It is, in fact, a way of life that carries with it the law of reciprocation. In other words, whatever you give as an impression will surely come back to you, whether it is a welcoming attention or neglect.

Many have missed out on so many good things of life because of lack of courtesy. Some have been rejected in contract bids; some have missed business opportunities, and some have destroyed relationships that would have been of great benefit to them because of something as simple as polite greeting.

This reminds me of a striking incident that occurred in my neighborhood in May 2012. It was the Spring season in full bloom and many families were out on the street with little clothing on, just to stay away from the heat inside and cool off outside with others. Talk about the next booty camp! The entire street seemed to be having a jamboree -children playing around with their bicycles, boys throwing about their basketball, men talking loudly and drinking beers and wines, and women dancing and chatting. Everywhere was simply bubbling with fun, as old school R & B music boomed from speakers, and people enjoyed themselves in every way they could.

I had just returned from work that interesting afternoon and, fortunately, my buddies – Daniel and Justus – were around too. The entire atmosphere was so lively that no one wanted to be inside. My friends and I and a few others sat on the stairs leading to the front door of a neighboring house. We soon started talking about the final leg of the football match between the Patriots and the Eagles and how it would end up with the Patriots winning. Just then, a Toyota Hilux van pulled into the street, with three men and a lady inside. I noticed the van was on a mission to the house we were in as the man in the front seat was pointing his fingers at it.

Almost immediately, the lady came out of the van and walked straight towards us. My neighbor, Ms. Smith, was very curious and kept asking me if I knew the visitors. I whispered that they must have come from the nearby church to visit their member who lived in the apartment we were standing on. I must admit that the lady looked gorgeous. Ms. Smith instantly suggested that she must be an executive of the church, seeing how smartly dressed she was. Incidentally, the family they were looking for were sitting in the garden where the music box was playing, oblivious of the visitors' arrival.

As the lady drew closer, we were getting set to welcome her and provide answers about the family's whereabouts and any other questions she might have. Shockingly, however, when she got to where we were, she just walked past us to the door, with a stern face and not a single word. I felt disappointed and, at the same time, embarrassed. I noticed the shock on everybody's face too, especially Ms. Smith. But I simply dismissed the lady's action as being a mere oversight. I even signaled to others not to be bothered.

Soon, we resume our discussions and acted like nothing heartbreaking had just happened. The lady knocked at the wooden door and pressed the bell for some minutes but did not get a response. Apparently fed up, she walked down to us and pompously disrupted our conversation with, "I came to meet the family in that apartment but there was no response. I have knocked the door and pressed the doorbell severally. Do you know their whereabouts, or can I just drop a message for you to help me deliver it to them?"

As if on cue, none of us responded. We continued with our discussions and completely ignored her. She was visibly embarrassed. She wanted to go but changed her mind to stay back

– probably with the intention of lashing out at us in anger or simply to beg us for a response. At that same moment, the other people in the van, sensing what was going on, came out and dashed towards us. The man who appeared to be the leader greeted us cheerfully and stretched out his hands for a handshake. That seemed to calm our nerves a bit.

Seizing this opportunity, the leader asked that since the family they came to meet was not at home, they would want to share a few words with us and invite us to their church. We all turned down the request because the initial signal we had gotten portrayed the group and their church as being disrespectful and untrustworthy.

Let me repeat: first impression matters because it lasts the longest. This is why it is rightly said that you never get a second chance to make a great first impression. Just a single uncivil attitude from that church lady had done enough to poison our minds towards her group and her church. Whereas, just a single "Hi" or "Hello" from her would have made a whole lot of difference and turned the tide in their favor because we had initially been captivated by her appearance! In fact, I was so sure that Ms. Smith was ready to walk her to where the family was relaxing, just by the corner of the street, and I was sure we would all have wanted to listen to their message, if only the lady had made a good first impression on us with a polite attitude. This shows that there is much in a greeting – you can win or lose a lot, depending on how you handle the possibilities embedded in it!

2
POWER OF YOUR MANNERS
"If we want to make friends, let's greet people with animation and enthusiasm."
- Dale Carnegie

The atmosphere at the local whole food store was as calm as that of any other day, with shoppers coming in and going out excitedly. Suddenly, everyone's attention was jolted to the hysterical yelling of an elderly woman, who was apparently furious at the cashier. Not only was she creating a huge scene with her voice, but she was also throwing fresh vegetables, fruits and whatever else she could lay her hands on at the hapless lady.

Everyone was confused as to what could have caused such aggravated hatred and bitterness toward such a good-looking lady behind the counter. Some people assumed that the two women must either had held unsettled grudges against each other from previous encounters or that the cashier must have said something very rude to the aged customer. Somehow, some other women on the queue managed to restrain the old woman so she could stop assaulting the young lady who had become so shaken that she was crying profusely. People asked the cashier what she had done to so provoke the customer and she replied, amidst sobs, that she had done nothing to her.

Well, while the young might have sincerely thought she had not transgressed, the elderly woman had a contrary opinion. According to her, the lady cashier had not only attended to her with a disrespectful attitude but had made things worse by rebuffing all attempts on her part to have a polite and friendly banter with her. "I respected her and smiled and tried talking to her, but she was too proud," the customer blurted out.

A Deeper Look

Of course, most people, including me, would consider the action of the old woman as being extreme but the truth is that people react in different ways to attacks on their personal dignity. To that elderly woman, the cashier's persistent refusal to be well-mannered, even when she, as the customer, had made the first move, meant that she (the customer) was being considered a nonentity and she wasn't going to let it slide.

The question is: Wouldn't things have been different, if the lady had, despite all the pressures or problems she might be going through, simply reciprocated the customer's friendly greeting, at least? This is why it is important that we understand the impact that our manners can have on others. When we treat people with respect, especially by properly greeting them or responding to their greetings, we are doing so much more to them and to ourselves than we can ever imagine. As a sociologist explains, "Truly noticing others is fundamental to their self-worth. We all need recognition. We need to feel that we matter. This does not mean that we should be running for glory and honor, but every human being has a basic and natural desire to be acknowledged as significant. And we can give some of this significance to others simply by greeting them properly."

I am sure you are beginning to have a better understanding of what happened at that neighborhood store. The needless uproar that took about an hour to resolve could have been avoided if the cashier had understood this fundamental principle of interpersonal interactions. She might have thought she was simply being "professional" – as many of us sometimes think. After all, why should she spend time talking with "strangers" who came to buy stuff from the store? And what did it matter whether she acknowledged the small gift of greeting coming from an old lady or not, since she was there for business?

But as we have already seen, acknowledging others matters a lot. Our immediate attitude and posture when we meet someone can either uplift or depress them. It can brighten or dampen their mood. And it can make them have either a positive or a negative disposition towards us. Indeed, there are people who go about with loads of psychological and emotional hurts. Perhaps all they need is just one more negative attitude from someone to trigger them to explode or a positive attitude from some to melt away the baggage of insecurity and anguish they are struggling to deal with. I tell you, reader, you can make a difference. We can make a huge difference!

The Essence
So, what exactly is the purpose of all we have been exploring so far? How essential is it to have good manners? Are we to greet others so we will not be accused of being insolent or disrespectful? Are we to acknowledge and return greetings so we do not get pelted with fruits and vegetables – or even stones – like the unfortunate cashier? Or maybe we should just be more respectful so that we do not miss our opportunities for promotion, favor, or some other privileges?

Well, all the above considerations are important. None can deny the fact that many people have lost valuable relationship and business opportunities – or even suffered worse misfortunes– simply by ignoring a little courtesy. However, I must emphasize that true courtesy is not shown with the motive of obtaining a favor, having a good reputation, leaving a good impression, or avoiding trouble. Courtesy is best shown out of love, respect, and humility.

As already emphasized, every human love to be recognized, respected, and appreciated. And indeed, everyone is important in their own way. The Golden Rule says, "do unto others as we desire them to do unto us". So, if we love to be respected and acknowledged, it should not be so difficult for us to do same to others. And of course, if we truly have genuine love and humility, we will not want to make others feel they are worthless or inferior to us. When we ignore this basic rule, then it is natural to expect things to go wrong.

I can tell you categorically that the bulk of the anger, outrage, and hostility we see all around us on daily basis is a consequence of belittling one another. Find out the cause of that quarrel between two people on the parking lot and you would realize that the simple rule of courtesy or good manners has been ignored and someone has felt belittled or ridiculed.

It can indeed be startling to discover why some of us fail to acknowledge others or why we feel they do not deserve respect. We see someone for the very first time and we conclude that they are too ugly, dirty, shabby, or smelly and therefore unworthy of our respect or being treated as a human being. Sometimes, it is the color of someone's skin, their language, accent or dressing that we use as a criterion that such are not worthy of being treated with consideration. And most times, the result is a buildup of tension or outright aggravation and conflict. We can avoid much of this by treating people with dignity through a welcoming smile, a disarming greeting, and a willing acknowledgement.

Business and Beyond
So far, we have established that greetings are important and vital to our daily living. We have realized that we can show love, make a good and memorable first impression and set a positive tone and mood for any conversation with whoever, whether a friend, spouse, boss, or client, anybody.

Beyond interpersonal relationships, however, it

must be noted that greetings and good manners generally can determine the success or otherwise of a business. In communicating with your customers, suppliers, staff, shareholders and others who are connected with your business - whether verbally or in writing– courteous greetings will go a long way in building a mutually beneficial relationship with them for a long time.

A warm, sincere greeting will touch the heart of the person you are relating with. No one can fake an attitude. No one can pretend to be true for long – sooner or later, the true color of a man or business manager will be known. People's instincts will sooner or later reveal to them whether you are genuinely concerned about their interest or you are only out to profit from them. Attitude is like the wind; you will always know if it is cold or warm.

A positive first impression will dissipate a customer's apprehension. The greeting is your chance to make a positive impression and set the tone for the entire buying and selling or business experience. Maybe the client does not want or need your product or service at that moment or is not considering buying from you. However, with a good seller-customer relationship in place through your honest and polite manners, you can change the course of things; you can persuade the customer to patronize you.

The truth is that customers sometimes do not buy a product because they prefer the brand to others; rather, they buy a product or service because of the relationship they have with the person or people behind it. Retired NBA Hall of Fame legend and business mogul, Earvin "Magic" Johnson (Jr.), captured this truth perfectly: "With businesses, you go to the same places because you like the service, you like the people and they take care of you. They greet you with a smile. That is how people want to be treated, with respect. That is what I tell my employees, "customer service is very important."

Indeed, a thoughtful message, a warm welcome, a kind smile, and a charming gesture can create a rethink and a spark for further conversation and bidding and interest in a product. The customer will always remember that someone made them have a beautiful experience and that will linger in their minds for a long time.

The key to good customer service is building good and lasting relationships with them, thanking the customer, and promoting a positive, helpful, and friendly environment will ensure they leave with a great impression. A happy customer will return often and is likely to spend more money and more time patronizing you, and more often tell other people to come taste and experience a family.

Good customer relationship starts with attitude and knowledge, it is all about bringing customers back, again and again, And sending them away happy and happy enough to pass a good and positive feedback and recommendation to the outside world, who may then try the product or service you offer for themselves and in their turn become customers.

Good attitude and interpersonal skill will turn you to a productive and successful businessperson, you can sell anything to anyone once you have built a spark through your charm and attitude. No matter what you sell or the kind of service you render, it will be your approach to how you relate with every individual first before considering the beauty and power of the product, the way you greet and approach a customer is what will determines whether or not you'll ever be able to sell that person anything else again. The essence of forming a relationship with greeting and good customer service is to win the people who might not have had any reason to take your product or service to consideration, the achievement of a successful business is – a relationship that the individual customer feels they have gotten that would likely bring them back.

How do you go about forming such a relationship? By remembering the one true secret of good customer service and acting; accordingly, "You will be judged by what you do and what you say, and what you put on the show glass".

If you truly want to have good customer service, interpersonal relationship that will turn a passer bye or a window shopper to a ferocious, committed and a die-hard customer, whose heart is stayed on your product before any other. All you have to do is ensure that your business, staff, and customer relation office consistently follows the rules of character, greeting and love

Job Hunting

In the summer of 2019, I was at the University of California, Berkeley, to attend the school's graduation ceremony for the Department of Administration and Human Resources. At the seminar for the graduating students, the Pro-Chancellor spoke with so much insight and enlightened the students about the rules of employment in the business world. He told them: "Remember that when you are going for an interview after school, seeking employment, you represent the campus. A good interview can leave a candidate with positive feelings and good expectations about his performance with the interviewer. Your performance is rated from the moment you step into the building gates. Your smile, you attitude and greetings towards the people you meet, your physical representation and comportment will be the reason the job is yours. That is the first mark you will earn; other aspects of the interview are secondary and are upshots of what you have learned in this great school.

"Who you are in their minds and how they will rate the school, even if you do not get a job offer, matters a lot. A bad interview, starting with a bad impression of you, may result in a bad reputation for the campus. The sole target of the interviewer is to reach your personality first and not your book knowledge. The book knowledge is important; and that is the area in which you compete with the rest of the applicants. The purpose of an interviewer is to gather information about the applicant's friendliness, empathy, fairness and reverence, coupled with his competencies and work experience, so that they can select the best qualified candidate."

The pro-chancellor continued, as he spoke to the graduating students on how to win the war outside, it is not by the level of parental influence and wealth or the letter of reference from a reputable individual which when sent will increase your chances to push you up to the top so you can get the job, but it all starts with been exceptionally kind and respectful to everyone you interact with during the interview process, wear a killer outfit that will depict your character and taste, arrive early enough to compose yourself before your interview starts, and ace the "Tell me about yourself" question that comes from the interviewer.

As you are set to leave the school into the Labor market, you meet a lot of competition and pressure to deal with the different kinds of people that will either uphold you to success or wanting to pull you down because of what you want that they also want, with many graduates competing for the same, limited amount of jobs, particularly in the creative industries, it's never been more crucial to stand out from the crowd and secure that first step onto the career ladder.

From the minute you walk into any job interview, the product you are selling is you, the information you are passing on to those on the square table is your character. So, you must act professionally as soon as you enter the company gate and throughout the interview process and leave a good impression. The more you impress the interviewer, the better chance you will have of securing the position. But how do you win them over? The following tips will help you get there.

The first thing you must all put as task is to work on your attitude, your attitude towards others and anyone you meet as you go about the process, you do not know who will be the ladder to getting you up to your next role, respect everyone, be kind and gentle, smile a lot and greet, the people and the company is primarily seeking for a good person that will project them as good and reputable organization.

Sidney James Weinberg said with tears as he became the CEO of a world class company, he invented Flamin' Hot Cheetos and became an executive of the PepsiCo after working as a janitor's assistant, making $3/week. My good attitude, respect for everybody got me to the echelon of success, I thought I was going crazy when the first thing I do every day is to greet, before starting my cleaning job, I greet everybody, I greet both small and big, old and young and I never stopped. It was my way of life, I never know who answered when I greet because that is not my concern, my concern is to share love and hope, and I never bothered to know who is qualified to be shown love, I just love everybody and I express this by greeting, no wonder I got help from the person I least expected.

Weinberg's background contrasted to that of the rich or of the Ivy League brought up, he was one of the 11 children born of his middle class immigrant parent, Sidney's name does not appear in any document after the world war 1, indicating that he was less an active person in his young life into adulthood, moreover, he was a drop out of junior school at age 13.

In his story, he met with Paul J. Sachs, the firm's founder, and CEO. Unknowingly as he worked as a Janitor at the prestigious investment banking enterprise, Goldman Sachs. He won the attention of the CEO with his smile, charm and good character, the firm's founder took notice of him, his work ethics, smiles and love for everybody, and got promoted to the mailroom, and that was the begging of his flight to the top. Sachs saw great potential in Weinberg, not from his academic excellence, and definitely not from his family background as the son of the rich and famous, but rather the very words he spoke to him that cold day, when Sachs was having troubles with his suitcase and the scattered documents and file on the stairways, Weinberg helped, gave a kind smile and gave me encouragement as we knelt down together gathering the flying papers, he greeted me so well and honorably without knowing who I am.

Family setting

The power of courtesy is also easily manifested within the home environment. Little thoughtful gestures, as well as words and attitudes that reflect respect, acknowledgements and gratitude can make a big difference between couples. Think about it; before marriage, you most likely showed a lot of good qualities, including a very respectful attitude towards the person you are with. This often is the case when people are still dating and planning to get married. There is usually so much fun, in an atmosphere of respect and mutual understanding. Unfortunately, however, for most couples, things begin to take another shape soon after marriage, as mutual understanding begins to fade and respect begin to fall off the eyes, they have seen all and known all, they are now too acquainted and familiar with each other that the passion and affection they started with begins to disappear and pride start taking its toll.

Many marriages start having troubles simply because the couple have lost some fundamental elements that should have kept the ball of love rolling. Valuing each other in a marriage is golden. This value can be best demonstrated and strengthened by putting love and respect at the forefront of the relationship. Such love and respect manifest through affectionate exchange of warmness, accolades, greetings and showers of unending communication, and the desire to uplift the other partner's mood always. You show how much you care in enthusiastic ways when you keep up with those warm greetings.

Let the tender and affectionate greetings start with you. Let it be what begins your day and let it continue throughout. Your spouse needs to know and feel that he or she is special to you at every moment and time, and the easiest way to give such assurance is by the way you address them. You can consider this a friendly reminder to you not to allow familiarity to sabotage the loving way you greeted and cared for each other before this time.

Do not take your spouse for granted. Be intentional in greeting him or her in a loving and caring way. This alone can deepen, strengthen, and fortify your relationship beyond your imaginations. When he or she enters the home after being gone for the day, show that you care. Do not wait to be greeted first; welcome him or her with much enthusiasm. It should not matter if there has been a misunderstanding before that time, or, maybe there was something you are not happy about before then. Just make them feel loved by your welcoming words. If this rule can be applied often, it will touch your spouse's heart and open the door to a refreshed intimacy between you two.

Show by your words and body language that you are glad your spouse has physically reentered your world again. Greet him or her with even more enthusiasm than you would greet other people. This is the least you can do for "the love of your life." And here is some additional advice given by Angie Makis: "And if you are the one coming home—find your spouse first, before your kids, before your dog, and certainly before your phone. Spouse first."

As a marriage counselor with a local church with Christ Embassy, my major concern has never been if the couple love themselves, because love does not totally guarantee that a marriage or relationship will not break up, love cannot help you stick to one partner, or that your partner will stick with you all through, and on the other hand, cheating isn't always a product of not loving your partner enough, in fact, loving someone does not guarantee they won't cheat or fall in love with someone else. Relationship work mostly because of what we kept in the head about our partner and marriage, that character, and personal commitment to want to make it work is the brainer, and that starts with the efforts and attitude that is added to it. Marriages and relationships work because of the emotional maturity, empathetic intelligence and self-discipline which is driven into the deepest part of the heart by our personal efforts and then begin to manifest from the stand point of mutual respect, respect that starts from greeting each other lavishly, using and giving gifts, cards, words of mouth that came from the heart, regular calls and messages to know how the other is faring for the day, esteeming one another and communicating much effectively. Time will come when they will begin to see even more handsome man or a more beautiful woman out there, a more romantic, intelligent, sexy, rich, curvy and God fearing person than the one we left at home or in a relationship with, in those times, self-discipline will be the help against the temptation.

Relationships are never a readymade, you must build it, and it is not just love that keeps the two together forever, though it is the driving force and indeed the fundamental, it is the determination and commitment, overlooking mistakes and wrongs and to be the one that gives the most when it is more challenging.

Everyone falls in love; it takes a little or no effort to do that, but staying in love is from building a relationship which comes from commitment to one another, discipline and respect that keeps it standing, and all these is culminated with greeting, it starts here.

Greeting to building a relationship is not only the 'good morning Honey" kind of thing, it is broad, it is addressing the other person with attention, sparking up conversation and involving each other in communication at every point, Almost every conflict in our marriage has been related to a lack of communication. When we are not communicating about both our outer and inner life with each other, we are headed for trouble. At the same time, our most mutual and meaningful moments have come from open and honest communication about everything from what happened in our day to what is going on in the deepest parts of our being.

Do not assume that your spouse knows what you are thinking and feeling, it is time to get together and talk about it. Do not be afraid to ask about anything either. If you are not sure what your spouse is thinking or feeling, ask them. That's the quickest way to find out what is needed and how you can be involved, because conversation starts from talking to each other even when there is a fault lurking underneath the curtain by the other person and it can easily be started by saying a word or greeting, relationships experience setback when they begin to restrain conversation and keeping information from each other because they do not have the spark to, trouble will begin to grow as soon as they begin to keep quiet and send a sensitive message of displeasure with what the other person had done wrong. The secret to having a happy marriage and lasting relationship is not because everything has been going smoothly in the kitchen and on the bed, even happy couples argue. Focus on each other's strengths. Do not expect your partner to be a 100% perfect angel. But still, do things together. Choose to be attracted to your spouse, Laugh with each other. Be kind to one another. Celebrate small, good, moments and start everyday well by greeting with words and gestures.

Report had shown that a higher percentage of women will prefer to ignore their man and not greet or pay serious attention to them as they arrive home from work or outing, or when they wake up in the morning after a quarrel or misunderstanding, in fact, they want to show their anger and displeasure of their man's wrong attitude by keeping malice, avoiding to greet or not greeting properly as they would if everything was going good. This attitude has pushed most of these vulnerable partners to anger and made them to misbehave when they are supposed to be loving, and which had led many homes to disarray. But if they would ignore all the offenses and push aside all the wrongs they may have had from their man, and just put on a kind smile, sweetness and warmness with greetings that sounds enchanting, they will be achieving a lot of winning.

The Scriptural Perspective

We now come to an especially important aspect of our discussion that I believe should further confirm to you the primacy and potency of greetings. To begin with, it is remarkably interesting to know that greeting is important to God. I mentioned previously that spiritually speaking, divine attention is granted to that worshiper who starts the day and every prayer made to God with intense praise and intense worship, which is a form of greeting to the Almighty. King David in Psalm 5:3 declares, "My voice shalt thou hear in the morning, O Lord; in the morning will I direct my prayer unto thee and will look up."

David was so sure that God would hear his prayers because he was used to greeting the heavenly Father by way of praise and worship. He was used to greeting the Heavenly father with accolades as his first obligation. In fact, in the verse preceding the one above, he calls the Lord "my King and my God". He will wake up in the morning and bow himself to greet, he will dance and shake himself as a way of esteeming Him, he will sing and laugh loud to show he is in love with his heavenly God, at every point he has the opportunity to communicate with God, he reverence and worships Him. No wonder, he found special favor with God and received nearly everything he wanted and more. From kingship to wealth, to fame and victories over nations that came against him in war, God gave him priority attention because he was a man of praise and worship who had built a great relationship with the Almighty over time.

It is a similar record we have of Abraham. In James 2:23, he is described as "the friend of God" because his life was devoted to acknowledging God's greatness and sovereignty. He put God before anything else, which was a powerful way of respecting him. Incidentally, to praise in Greek terminology is to greet, to hail or to acknowledge as high and awesome, which was what Abraham did throughout his life.

It was also said of Adam and Eve that God would usually come to the garden in the cool of the day to have communion with them (Genesis 3:8). God was searching for Adam in the garden that faithful day, and knew something was amiss, ordinarily, Adam would come out and greet His Supremacy and bow before Him and shower words of praise and adoration which is that greeting we are talking about, but at this time he was nowhere to be found, that greeting, that praise, that adoration was missing and God knew it, He felt something was wrong that morning and so He kept searching for Adam until he was found and queried. This could happen because they had built a good relationship with each other overtime, with greetings and communication through Adam's reverential attitudes, as well as acknowledgment of God's supremacy.

How did I come about this? Well, we particularly know that Adam knew the power of greetings, especially with the way he acknowledged the wonders of the wife God gave to him. As soon as God presented Eve to him, he declared, "This is now bone of my bones, and flesh of my flesh: she shall be called Woman, because she was taken out of Man" (Genesis 2:23). This spontaneous romantic poem that Adam composed for his wife was not only to serenade her but also to acknowledge and appreciate God who had given her to Him.

The attitude of God's angels in particular – who are messengers of God – should give you an insight into the importance that God wants us to attach to greetings in our relationship with Him and our fellow men. If you look through the Scriptures, you will find that whenever an angel was to deliver a message to the people of God, he often started with a greeting – regardless of the fact that angels are below humans, because humans are the express image of the Almighty

God. For instance, the angel who came to Gideon greeted him and called him a "mighty man of valor" (Judges 6:12). The one who came to Daniel told him, "O Daniel, a man greatly beloved" (Daniel 10:11).The one that came to Mary said to her, "Hail, -greeting, thou that art highly favored, the Lord is with thee: blessed art thou among women" (Luke 1:28). And, most importantly, the angels that announced the birth of Jesus Christ, greeted the shepherds that watch over their flock by night and declared, "Glory to God in the highest, and on earth peace, good will toward men" (Luke 2:14).

Even Jesus shows us the power of greeting in building relationship with the way he handled Nathaniel, the brother of Philip. Nathaniel had been so skeptical and cynical about the announcement of the Messiah that he famously said, "Can any good thing come out of Nazareth?" (John 1:46). Yet, when Jesus met Nathaniel, he did not condemn him; instead, He gave him a welcoming greeting that completely disarmed him! He said, "Behold an Israelite indeed, in whom there is no guile!" (John 1:47). That made the heart of Nathaniel to easily open to Him.

57

Finally, we learn the power of greeting from Paul the Apostle. That man had so much influence on the early church because, apart from everything else, he knew how to greet and acknowledge the people to whom he addressed his words. Check out all his epistles and you will find him beginning with a special greeting. Even while addressing the Corinthian Christians whom he was not happy with and was soon to heavily chastise, he started by first greeting them, saying, "Grace be unto you, and peace, from God our Father, and from the Lord Jesus Christ" (1 Corinthians 1:3).

You too can build a wonderful dimension of relationship with God and your fellow men with your greetings.

The Communal Angle
Greeting has a big impact on not just our lives but the communities we belong. I once read a journal article about the Ife and Modakeke communal clashes, and that triggered my interest in the primary cause of the hostilities between these two communities. Incidentally, the protracted crisis, which began many years ago, had, as at the time of my fact-finding,

taken the lives of over 12,000 people and caused wanton destruction of properties of both the warring indigenes and other settlers.

Very few people have bothered about the cause of this war, so let me give you a little background. You see, these two communities are of the Yoruba ethnic group and they are both in present-day Osun State in Southwestern Nigeria. The socio cultural and political systems of the two communities are essentially identical and their geographical distributions largely overlap. Despite these shared attributes, their mutual animosity, which has dragged for over a century, is regarded by many historians as the oldest intra-ethnic conflict in Nigeria.

It is believed that the hostilities began when a chief from Modakeke allegedly refused to greet a chief from Ife, when both met at an event organized by some British travelers who had come to establish missionary works and build water systems in the region. Since the projects were supposed to benefit both communities, the chiefs and some other dignitaries from both sides had been invited and they had stayed together throughout the occasion, drinking, and eating together. In fact, it is said that they had sat side-by-side discussing the developments that were about to happen in their communities.

As the event ended, however, the Ife chief got angry that the Modakeke chief did not greet him with a bow before leaving the event as tradition dictated. That was how the blaze of anger and hatred was kindled– which rapidly led to an explosion of simmering tensions and grievances. From these two leaders, the indigenes of the communities began to despise one another. Faults began to grow and, inevitably, questions about who originally settled in the region and who really owned the lands, rivers, factories, schools and other resources and facilities that both had hitherto shared began to arise. Of course, as bitter hatred became the order of the day, the situation soon got out of hand, leading to many casualties and destructions, before it was eventually contained. However, the cracks and the scars of the strained relationship still linger.

The Ife and Modakeke crises has lasted over a century now, it remains the oldest intra ethnic conflict in Nigeria, the long rivalry continued as lands, boundary disagreements, migration and settlement issues began to grow and spread, and more hatred among those two tribes, this would not have happened if they had settled themselves with that little aspect of greeting,

In the same way, many other communities, associations, and groups that should have been collectively productive and prosperous together have been plunged into irreparable crisis, simply because of bad manners and disrespect for greeting which in most cases is the base for some laws and order in a community or state. From what we have seen so far, therefore, we can sum up the power of greetings as follows:

- Greetings will deliver a positive impression of you and your personality to anyone that meets you. Your attitude to greetings reveals your mindset and philosophy of life. If you have a proper perspective of life, with a good appreciation of the diversity in human nature, cultures and circumstances, greeting wouldn't be a problem for you; but

61

if otherwise, you will surely make a big deal out of it.

- Greetings can help you to positively affect the lives of everyone you come across and it can facilitate your progress and promotion in life too. Greetings do not only help you in maintaining a good social image but also help you in your professional life (We will explore the significance of this professional aspect later).

- Greetings can help to reveal your real personality to others. From a simple first word of mouth and the way you give yourself to humility which usually comes from greetings, your personality can be revealed. Therefore, most corporate organizations now hire with the "transparent window" approach. They start their interview with a prospective employee from the reception window - from his gesticulations to his communication style. What did he communicate and how did he communicate it? Did he smile? They want to know if he greeted rightly and at the right time and who he greeted. Did he, for instance, greet the janitor cleaning the floor or did he acknowledge the person sitting next to him, did he greet because the person standing next to him is well dressed and looking corporate?

Truth is that, sometimes, the Human Resources team plants different categories of people in the interview room. Those who appear like top management staff and those who seem to belong to the lower cadre are made to sit, work, or lurk around the place. The goal is to see how the jobseekers relate with the people they meet. The 21st century hire professionals started the transparent window approach to add to their recruitment techniques, using the "greet" criterion as the primary source of their first impression about the job applicants whom they are looking forward to employ in their organizations.

- Greetings could be a signpost to your place of origin, beliefs, and ideologies. Yes, the way you greet will tell where you come from and the kind of family upbringing you have received. Recent studies show how cultural values reveal a person's identity, ethnicity, race, and nationality. Many traditions believe that greeting is a law that must be adhered to, and if flouted, can call for a strong penalty to the offender; some, however, do not place much emphasis on it.

- Greetings, in a way, could douse tension or reduce the possibility of strife. In families or other settings where there are prolonged conflicts, it is often because none has diligently applied the principle and power of greetings. So, no one wants to apologize or say something of a good will to the other. However, if someone could apply the power of proper greeting, especially with a touch of sincerity, humor and thoughtfulness, it can lessen the hurt done to someone earlier and could ease up the tension and dispel the cloud of anger.

Good greeting habit will help you to easily get along with other people. Greeting is a human activity universally shared in any society and it is the only way to live peacefully with other people. Some people find it hard to make friends. It may be difficult getting to relate with someone you are meeting for the first time. Things can become easy however if you can take the initiative to acknowledge and greet them. It may not be easy to get acquainted with people we meet for the first time, but we can learn to get into people's lives by modesty and reverence.

- Greeting is also a way to know whether you are welcome or not. Usually when your greeting is not returned or when someone is not extending their greeting to you, it could be a clear sign that you are not wanted in that place. Your gesture being rebuffed could mean that something is wrong somewhere. Maybe there is a grudge that needs sorting out. You might want to consider leaving the place or applying another approach to create a rapport or using another method of greeting so you can pacify the individual.

- Greeting sets the tone for communication. As earlier said, the kind of relationship we build with people often depend on how we started with them in the first place. For instance, once a bad first impression has been given, it becomes hard to trust a person and give room for further acquaintances. Relationship could continue afterwards but it might be tense.

Now, it is important to know that how we say our greeting is as important as the greeting itself. Based on our inflection or emphasis on certain words, our body language and facial expressions, anyone can easily tell whether we are sincere or not ready for friendship at all. Simply put, the tone of our greeting conveys our attitude towards each other. Sometimes, we see people meeting for the first start, discussing enthusiastically, as if they had known each other for years. It is often because good impressions about tone and motive have been established from the beginning.

So, just as there are many forms of communication, so also are various tones that can go along with the messages. Sometimes what is ultimately communicated has nothing to do with the actual words used.

Most importantly, your greeting is a means of expressing love, care, warmth, and friendliness. People will not naturally want to open to strangers but the universally accepted way to break down the barriers of doubts and bring people into friendship is sincere greeting.

3
CULTURAL AND PROFESSIONAL COLORATIONS

"What I've realized is that the joy of meeting and greeting people from all around the world is universal."
- Joe Gebbia

I once read an interesting story about Thomas Jefferson, author of the Declaration of Independence. It was narrated that, one day, he and his eldest grandson were riding in a carriage together. As they proceeded, they met a slave who respectfully took off his hat and bowed. The President, according to his invariable custom, returned the salutation by raising his hat. However, the young man with him paid no attention to the slave's greeting. Mr. Jefferson, after a moment's pause, turned a reproachful eye to his grandson and said, "Thomas, do you permit a slave to be more of a gentleman than yourself?"

One striking observation I want you to make in the above narration is that, while it is possible that the younger Jefferson was being deliberately haughty towards the slave, it is also possible that he didn't respond to the slave's gestures of greeting because he hadn't attached much importance to such gestures or reciprocating same. This, inevitably, attracted the displeasure of the older man.

The reality is that many of us sometimes make the same mistake as the young man, especially when relating with people of other cultures. We sometimes either ignore certain cultural nuances that have to do with courtesy and greeting or we underestimate their significance. And naturally we offend sensibilities or run into even more serious trouble.

There is, indeed, no doubt that the world is changing and quickly becoming a global hut from being a "global village", as initially coined by Marshal McLuhan. People travel everywhere and meet people of different cultures and beliefs, with different ideologies. Many have gotten into trouble because they do not know what is not acceptable to a particular people or in a place.

Greetings around the world differ radically from culture to culture and sometimes they are shaped by religion or even superstitions. Knowing how to greet someone when visiting another country, culture or environment can help you avoid an awkward or problematic encounter.

Shades of Greetings around the world

It will interest you to know how greetings define people's lives in different parts of the world and how they relate with people outside their sphere. We will see different ways on how people greet in different countries and cultures and how you may fit into it, probably when you find yourself visiting or staying there. A good many of the meetings with the different people and culture may be baffling if you are not well acquainted with these ways and cultures, the thought of getting friendly and winning more people to your side will be the reason why you will want to understand a few more system around the world:

- In **Argentina,** people greet one another with a kiss to the cheek, irrespective of the age or gender. They do this to show warm acceptance and readiness to relate. So, do not be surprised or offended if this occurs. Lightly pressing your cheek against the right cheek of another for a light kiss is both formal and informal and it will not hurt at all and it does not depict any sexual implication even to the opposite sex. This form of greeting as they usually stand close to each other when they are having conversation and you may want to adjust and release yourself, else, you may be pushing the warmth of a good welcome and acceptance.

- In modern **Japanese tradition,** the common way of greeting for men and women is to bow, and that has been on from the beginning of this tradition, as opposed to giving a casual handshake or a hug. The first time I saw this was in a movie and I wondered and thought about this method of greeting, it would have been thought that it is the conventional fight greeting method

71

before it begins. Also, this tradition of bowing is the same in all ages - the young bow and the elder will do likewise but the levels of the bow may differ. I studied the trend for a while and noticed that the younger bow first and the other follows in like manner. The head to the waist region is slightly bent facing downwards and the hands are held together as if to pray. If you did not know, it might offend you to see someone bow and expecting you to do likewise.

- In some parts of **Nigeria**, West Africa, young people usually greet each other in a special way. They end their handshake with a snap of their fingers. This means that a handshake is not complete if the snap does not follow. Besides, it might take up to two or three times to rub the hands in a certain way until the finger snapping takes place; so, you may need to be taught the process. This form of greeting is most common among the **Igbo** tribe. Both the young and the old are allowed to shake hands and snap the fingers and in addition use the back of their hands to hit each other's hands three times or sometimes use a walking stick to hit each other's stick three times. Women are also allowed to go through that process, depending on the relationship.

- The **Yoruba** tribe, in that same Nigeria, have their own way of greeting, which is sometimes seen by others as a bit extreme. To show respect for authority and seniority, the males are meant to prostrate, they fall forward with both hands touching the ground, while the legs are thrown backwards, such that the stomach will flatten out and could touch the ground. The female folks are required to kneel, making sure each knee touches the ground and their head is slightly bowed. In addition to this, traditional rulers are meant to be greeted with the man's cap and the female head gears taken off as the fellow begin to greet, otherwise, there will be grave punishment.

Many other tribes and cultures are beginning to welcome this method of greeting as they accept the fact that it differentiates the older from the younger, the rich from the poor and the leader to the follower which makes social respect and cultural value a blessing.

- So in **Kenya,** among the Masai tribe, the joy of jumping up so high is a sign of welcome and acceptability, just like when a new member is introduced into the clan or community, the warriors of the Maasai tribe form a circle and jump as high as possible, this is particular with the Maasai clan, and to the general view of greeting in Kenya as the modern age appears further, Sometimes, when a person meets another person around town, or for a meeting, they hold hands close to the elbow for about three seconds, saying words of greeting like the word "Hujambo" and acknowledging one another. This also is a sign of approval and welcome. When you visit this neighborhood, don't be embarrassed when they begin to jump, it is a sign of approval and warmth and do not forget to extend your elbow for a grip, the hand shake may not be handy at most instance.

- Known as **Hongi**, the traditional Māori

greeting in **New Zealand** is done by pressing your nose and forehead to another person's nose at the same time. This is a greeting typically done with those you are close with. To perform it, you place your nose and upper lip against the cheek or forehead of the other person and take a breath. Many of the descents will prefer to go with the way they are been brought up in the traditional Hongi style instead of that of the western world, where they shake hands or kiss the cheek

- The **Wai tribe in Thailand** will place their palms together at the chest region and bow the heads lightly so that the thumbs touch the chin. The greeting consists of a slight bow with the palms pressed together in a prayer like fashion. Looking at this form of greeting, it revolves around their religious belief and has its origin from the Indian Anjali Mudra.

Learning more from indigenes of the Wai, it is just a way to prove that the visitor is not holding a weapon as some visitors had disguised as friends but attacked them and took their lands and women, this belief has dated back as the 12th century where all Wai will show the hands to the face, fixed together. The higher the clipped fingers go the more respectable the person you are greeting is, for slightly more respect, your finger climbs to the tip of your nose from the normal level of the chin. For people of higher standing, the finger moves higher to the forehead region and to the chiefs, religious leaders and royalties, the finger touches the hairline.

- **French nationals**, including children, shake hands with their friends and any other person they are with, and often kiss them on both cheeks, both upon meeting and leaving. The common greeting in **France** is kissing on the cheek. Typically, it will be two kisses, one on both cheeks, but the number of kisses can vary, depending on the region. As a common starting point, offer your right cheek and let the other person lead.

    Shaking of hands is common, when meeting a person for the first time, and when it looks formal and the person might not be of same religion and cultural understanding like meeting an Arab woman, they wait to receive the person's gesture and the way they wish to greet and be greeted before they continue.

- **In India**, greeting is carried out by placing your hands together in a praying position, just like the Wai tribe in Thailand, with your fingers pointed upwards and bowing slightly, then you say "Namaste." This is typical of the Hindus. There are some other methods of greetings with the Punjabi and the Tamil people of Rajasthan.

  India has 28 States and with hundreds of different cultures amalgamation of several various cultures, religion and tradition from around the region, and so, it may be difficult to stamp the particular style of greeting, but be assured that the warm welcome of this people is overwhelming. Placing both hands in prayer like position and as if you are about to pray, you might want to put a smile and say the words of greetings as the tradition dictates.

- **In Ukraine**, it is not allowed to pull back

after a kiss on each cheek. Here, the custom is to kiss the cheeks three times — left, right, left— to say hello. Often, they greet each other with a warm handshake with direct eye contact and words of greetings proceeding, a brief hug comes into way too, and with a pat on the back especially to people of the same sex and deeper relationship

- The **Chinese** tend to be more conservative. When meeting someone for the first time, they would usually nod their heads and smile, or shake hands if in a formal situation. But the **Tibet tradition in China** is so fundamental. It has to do with sticking out the tongue slightly as a way of telling the other person that there are no evil intentions within. This tradition dates to the 9th century and references the Tibetan king, Langdarma, who was known for his evil ways and had a black tongue. People still greet each other this way till today to show that they do not have the black tongue, characteristic of the tyrannical king. This style of greeting in Tibet may seem offensive to people from other countries, since sticking out the tongue is often used to boo in many places. But as already noted, in Tibet, it is the acceptable way of greeting; and, in fact, such gesture brings peace and understanding.

- In the **Philippines**, when greeting, the younger person takes the right hand of the elder person and pressing the knuckles against their forehead as a sign of respect and a way of requesting a blessing especially when the person is a religious leader or royalty, this they call the honoring-gesture. The usual greeting on the street is a handshake, both formal and informal and on the streets, but when it comes to tradition and respect, bring up the right hand of the person up to touch your forehead

- **In the United States of America**, it is normal for people to shake hands when they meet, but it is quite unusual for men to kiss when they greet each other. Greetings are usually casual with a handshake, a smile and a "hello" but can be more if the individuals are close acquaintances, they can hug and sometimes kiss the cheek. However, a simple "hello" is fine most of the time. Most greetings among the young men comes with a tough grip of the hands and pulling each other close to the body and sometimes with a pat on the back. The different gesture among young men and women is plenty, the different kinds of handshake and knuckle pop, where the back of the hands when held together like a punch precedes a handshake

- By tradition, **in Armenia**, especially in the rural areas, a woman needs to wait for the man to offer his hand for a handshake before she continue with her greeting, this is a way to show respect for their men as the head. Between good friends and family members, a kiss on the cheek and a light hug are also common.

This descendants from Greek are highly cultured and portrays respect and value to leadership and hierarchy, and that is why the young will not bring out the hands to greet until the elder initiates it.

- **The British** often simply say "hello" when they meet friends, they shake hands with a strong grip and often with a smile to reassure the other person of their acceptance. A peck on the cheek is common in informal situations among men and women and between members of the same gender who know each other very well.

- **In Arab countries**, close male friends or colleagues hug and kiss both cheeks. They shake with the right hand only for longer but less firmly than in the West. Contact between the opposite genders in public is considered obscene. Do not offer to shake hands with the opposite sex. The handshakes too are made with the fingers touching the chest, like how it is done in Malaysia.

- In **Saudi Arabia**, a handshake is followed by touching the chest, and most times a kiss to the cheek will be added, the women could hold and kiss another lady on the cheek but never with a male, this is against the law and punishable by the decrees established by the Government, there is strict gender segregation and it is sanctioned by the State and society, men and women will not greet each other in public or getting close to want to touch, hold or hug, except within close family and relations and to a husband and wife relationship only.

- When visiting Malaysia, remember to smile when you greet or come in contact with them as this is their way of life, the smile is the start of their relationship with you, Malaysian greeting consists of holding the palm of the hands and placing them against their heart, this gesture means: "I greet you from the bottom of my heart" and that is what they mean literarily. You may see Malaysians holding both hands like a double handshake, they often do this when saying goodbye to each other and often with the word "Salaam". men do not usually will shake hands with a woman, unless the woman extends the hands to allow the man to greet her in such manner.

- A **Hungarian** man who is cultured and with tradition will want to bow to an older person, this is a sign of respect but not common amongst the younger generation. Both male and female greet by shaking hands and may last for a few seconds as the continue with the usual verbal greetings, a man will not want to extend the hand to a woman for a handshake, rather will wait to see if the woman extends her hands before he can continue with such action. They would like to use the friendly greeting form of kissing each other on the cheeks just as they shake hands. The most common way is to kiss from your right to your left. When men meet for the first time, the casual norm is a firm handshake.

- In **Belgium**, people kiss on one cheek when they meet, regardless of the gender or how well they know each other. The Flemish greet most of the time with a handshake and always with the right hand, looking straight into the eyes of the person you are greeting, this way, you get more acquainted and become more friendly with each other. This is the same with the French speaking part of Belgium, they all shake hands with eyes gazing on each other and sometimes with a kiss on the cheek which may be up to 3 times, to the right cheek, then to the left and finally to the right.

- In **Russia**, the typical greeting is a very firm handshake, almost like you are trying to crush each other's knuckles, all the while they maintain direct eye contact. When men shake hands with women, the handshake is less vigorous as the respect that they are female is considered. It is also considered gallant to kiss women three times while alternating cheeks, and even to kiss hands.

- In **Albania**, men shake hands when greeting one another. Depending on how close the men are with each other, a kiss on each cheek is common as well. When a man meets a female relative, a kiss on each cheek, or two per cheek, is common. With friends or colleagues, normally a light handshake will do. Women may shake hands or kiss each other on both cheeks.

- There is something unique about **Zimbabwean** and **Mozambique's** cultural way of greeting, these Southern African countries have this applause style as part of their hello, in Zimbabwe, the clapping of hands comes when folks meet with each other, the first person who is the greeter claps once and the one responding to the greeting will clap twice. This is a form of showing approval and a warm welcome. The men have a different way by which they clap their hands to that of the women, the men clap with fingers aligned on the palm of the other hand, tapping it once as first greeter and tapping twice as responder, while the female clap with their hands at an angle, palm on palm. Similarly, in Mozambique, people clap their hands, but three times before they say "moni", (hello). Following this process as a visitor in these countries will tell that you are a part of their belief and you want to be a part of them. This will allow you to quickly blend with their community and enjoy their friendship.

- **Greenland and Tuvania** (Oceania) also have this greeting method that is sensational, Sniffing and allowing the smell of someone you love or want to be friend with get into the system of the body.

In Greenland which is the world's largest island, located between the Arctic and Atlantic oceans, the Kunik, that is the Inuit tradition, they place the nose and upper lip against someone's cheek or forehead and sniff for a few seconds. Though, this happens mostly with people that are known or relations, but on the South Pacific Island of Tuvalu, pressing cheeks together and taking a deep breath to enjoy the feeling and warmness is a vital part of a traditional way of welcoming visitors.

- The **Greek** custom allows for those greeting each other to tap the shoulder gently as they shake hands. This gesture reveals the warmness of their heart. Moreover, they claim it brings some assurance that the other person approves of the warmth of their greeting. A handshake is the common way to greet anybody, formal or informal, close friends may greet each other with a warm hug or and a kiss on the cheek, eye contacts are maintained which depicts they are trying to connect with emotions and seriousness.

Of course, a full list of how greeting is done in the countries of the world would be extensive, as each country differs just a little bit in the way they greet each other. Before visiting a foreign country, therefore, it is recommended to check on the various meanings of the way they greet and the gestures that follow, as a visitor may inadvertently find himself in a very unpleasant situation if he is not familiar with the rules.

The Professional Angle

It is pertinent and interesting to know that while culture and location are critical considerations in greetings and manners, contextualizing your greetings is also another essential issue to consider. Context here refers to setting; formal or informal, social, or professional. Since it is much easier to manage the social or informal context – considering that it is more natural and has indeed been our major focus from the beginning – I will be dwelling more on the formal or professional setting here.

Regardless of the country of the world in which we find ourselves, there are situations that require more formal or professional (business) language to communicate and send messages, including greetings. Formal messages and greetings are strictly professional and are mainly used for work purposes or business and corporate situations. They are characterized by a strict compliance with rules that indicate one's seriousness and level of exposure to the etiquette of the business environment.

Basically, we use formal greetings in business meetings and negotiations, at job interviews, in communicating with high-level management personnel of a company, showing respect to elderly individuals or people we do not know well, meeting new business colleagues, as well as communicating with the different categories of clients.

In these situations, we use more formal or professional language to show respect, to show the importance of the situation to the person or to keep a professional tone.

"Good morning", "Good afternoon", "Good evening" are the most common forms of greeting in a formal situation and they can be used with colleagues, business clients, new neighbors, and so on. To be particularly respectful, you can also include the person's last name, for example: "Good morning, Mr. Jones." If you know someone well (that is, if there is some level of familiarity), you can also use their first name. And when it comes to correspondence, writing a formal letter will require you to write, "Dear Sir", or "Dear Madam"; or better still, write, "Dear (the person's last name)" if you know it.

When you are greeting a group of people for example at a meeting, you can also use such expressions as "Good morning, everyone", "Hello. How do you do?" And it is expected you get a reply of "How do you do?" from the responder. It could also go along the same path as the "How are you?" question. This is a quite simple, polite, and appropriate question to use when you want to start a conversation in a business or formal situation.

In greeting friends, family, or colleagues you know well or clients you have developed a relationship with, it is okay to be a little more relaxed with the language. It is often also quite common to shake hands with someone when you greet them. This is common for business contacts and acquaintances.

"Hello" and "Hi" are common and appropriate to use in more informal situations. Most times, it is expected to add the person's first name - "Hello, Susan", "Hi, Larry" – since this further shows familiarity and friendliness. "Hey" is especially reserved for people that are close to you. It is the most informal of the greeting styles we have examined so far. Also note that "Hey" and "Hey there" are most often used among younger people or with peers. This kind of greeting is not appropriate with one's parents or other older persons or even superiors at work.

Most of the time, we use "Hello" or "Hi" with one of these questions: "How are you?", "How are you doing?", "How is it going?" These questions, in a strictly formal setting (especially when relating with those you are not familiar with) should have quite simple answers and should be more neutral: "Fine, thanks. And you?" Great! You?" "Doing well. And how have you been?" Not bad. And you?"

Sometimes, though, in a business setting, the answer is the same as the question, especially "How do you do?" This is often confusing the first time you hear it or experience it. What you must bear in mind is that the "question" is a form of greeting and not a real question. Therefore, it is most used when passing or walking by someone you know but have no time to talk to.

Slang greetings can change from country to country, region to region and even city to city. Slangs may sometimes seem abusive, but they are easy and friendly ways to express oneself in close relationships. Slangs bring people together even closer because they are forged from a common identity and experience. It is, however, important to learn which slang may be appropriate or understood in the region you are in or the people you are communicating with. For instance, using "Good day" is generally understood as an Australian greeting. It will sound strange to an American if you use this.

Hi / Hey / Hey there / Hey man, these are all common ways of saying "hello" with friends and family, just to make closeness with one another.

"Hi" can be used to casually greet people you know well or if you are meeting someone for the first time at a party, for example. However, "hey" is used with people you already know. "Hey" and "Yo" are most often used among younger people or with peers, this kind of greetings is not appropriate with parents or with one's grandparents and senior or respected persons.

"Hey man" is used among males and "hey dude" is a similar example. The casual way for those in the Military could sound strong and strange. Though it is Military slang, they are professional to their act. "Oorah", "Hahooha".

4
BUILDING LASTING RELATIONSHIPS

"Meet anger with sympathy, contempt with compassion, cruelty with kindness. Greet grimaces with smiles. Forgive and forget about finding fault. Love is the weapon of the future."

- Yehuda Berg

Some years ago, a young man who was an assistant doorkeeper at the Capitol in Washington overheard a stranger ask the doorkeeper for help in finding one of the senators from California. Obviously in a bad mood, the doorkeeper answered the stranger in a very disrespectful way that it was none of his business where the senators were.

Despite the stranger's repeated pleas, the doorkeeper would not budge. "I have trouble enough looking after the representatives," he insisted. Dejected and perplexed, the visitor from California turned to go. Just then, the young assistant doorkeeper ran to him and got his attention with a warm greeting, good morning sir, with a charming smile. Thereafter, he said, "If you are from California, you must have come a long way, I overheard your conversation with my boss, I will try to help you." Then he asked him to take a seat and hurried off in search of the senator.

Soon, the young man returned with the senator. The stranger was delighted. In appreciation, he gave his card to the young doorkeeper and asked him to call at his hotel that evening.

As it turned out, that stranger was none other than Collis Potter Huntington, the great industrialist who was arguably the most famous member of the "Big Four" that financed the Central Pacific and helped to create the Transcontinental Railroad. He came to the hotel to finalize plans with the Government representative – the Senator, about buying the hotel they were on.

When the doorkeeper called upon him that night, Mr. Huntington offered him a position three times the salary he was then receiving. He accepted the new position with tears and joy and became the new boss at the Hotel security division, he did well at his job and developed a great relationship with the industrialist. He was rapidly promoted from that time on. His testimony at the opening session of the Domino security training for the hotel security staff was enlightening; been good to others, no matter who they are and what they look like is the start of doing better good for yourself. I assisted Mr. Huntington that fateful evening, not because he looked rich or commanded me to. I could have kept away or pretended not to see him as he looked around for help, he was looking exactly like my grandfather at the farm, a faded brown shirt on an overall denim jeans and a papa's cap on his shining grey hair. He never looked who he is, but I never looked at what I saw before I did the right thing.

Getting it Right
Greeting people, as we have previously noted, goes beyond the routine wishes for a beautiful day; it encompasses all the thoughtful ways in

which we make them feel important, dignified, and beloved. It is, no doubt, what will give the first impression about you when you speak. Therefore, you must send a clear message that you care about every relationship by starting on the right foot, being courteous, and showing respect. Relationships with people are not sprints or marathons, but journeys. They are long-term investments that must be nurtured.

Here, we will examine some areas in which we can work on with our relationships with people. You can build strong and long-lasting friendships with people with your manners and attitude. You can win people's love and respect and at the same time make a lasting impression of goodwill on them. Let us see how to do this.

1. **Show them You Care**

As our opening story shows, at least, once in your lifetime, there is going to be someone who needs you or who needs your help. Maybe they are stranded or confused. Maybe they fell into that horrible pit of despair, or something terrible happened to them. Whatever the reason, if you need to show someone you care, and build their trust on you, this guide is for you.

- Ask how they are and how their day went. Don't just ask "How was your day?" at random. Make sure you genuinely want to know. People can tell if you are being sincere. If someone tells you that they had a great day, continue with letting them know you are happy for them. If they had a bad day, offer to comfort them. That alone will create a lasting impression and make you win their trust and love.

Imagine yourself in this situation. You had a bad day, and someone asked how your day was. You then explain to them why it was such a struggle and they ask if you want a hug. You would likely feel better. You can do the same thing in helping others. Everyone needs help at times. Everyone needs genuine help and friendship. If someone is carrying a heavy load of groceries, see if you can assist. If you see someone with depression or anxiety written all over them, lift the person's spirits and comfort them. Helping people undoubtedly boosts relationships and is known to elevate your mood.

- Pay attention to what the person really needs. This is often the hardest, but most important way to show you care. Even if they are just telling you a story about something silly that happened at the supermarket, it is important that you respond appropriately so that the other person senses you are genuinely interested. If you dismiss or ignore them when it comes to simple things, they will not feel that you care about them. Therefore, they are much less likely to share anything deeper with you in the future.

- Consider the person's likes or dislikes. What would they like you do with and for them? Try to study the person's moods and behavior. Some people like you to smile more when you are around them. This will make them more comfortable being with you, while some may desire you to create a first greeting and overture. If you notice someone who will want you to reach out to them more often, it is an indication that they want more closeness. Yet, there are some who may not like you getting too close to them. It might not be because they detest you or hate your person, but they may be too shy to get around people too quickly; or they may not like you to see their deficiencies. You can consider giving them their space and reaching them whenever and wherever it is most convenient for them to mingle with you.

Do they like to have their space all to themselves alone or do they like talking to themselves without having anyone intrude? What is their preferred method of communication? Are you listening to them? They may have some challenges hanging on their neck; they may be going through some difficulties that are making them act the way they are doing. If you can find time to hear them out, ask them why they do not respond appropriately the way you think they should and find a way to help them solve it. What are their passions? Please, find out. Listen to them if they want to talk. While some people are quiet after a difficult event, others will want someone to talk to. Make yourself available to them if they need a sympathetic ear and be sure to listen to their issues. Do not feel like you need to have any answers or solutions – just listening is often enough.

Many relationships tend to start out as a social connection and thereafter evolve into a business partnership or marital union. So, get to know people beyond the routine "hi". Engage them deeper and do it genuinely. They will remember that later.

2. **Walk in Their Shoes**

We need others, just as they need us. Helping them now will not only lift their spirits but will also connect you to your destiny helpers too.

Notice when someone is feeling down. Showing you care means paying attention to your friend's mood and asking if they are okay when they seem blue. Ask if everything is okay, if you can do anything for them, or what the problem may be. Signs that someone is unhappy include: Moodiness, self-isolation, irritability, lethargy and sometimes loss of appetite.

Place of Emotional Intelligence

Emotional intelligence is a critical factor in building lasting relationships and making indelible impacts in the lives of others.

Emotional intelligence is the ability to understand and manage your own emotions, and those of the people around you. So, aside from self-awareness, it also encompasses ability to understand other people's moods and why they act the way they do at certain times. Someone can be so rude this minute and be so generous with love the next minute. It all has to do with the ebb and flow of emotions. That capacity to be aware of, control, and express your emotions, as well as to navigate interpersonal relationships with both good judgement and empathy.

Most people react to others based on the way they feel inside of themselves. There are people who have internal struggles, battles, challenges, questions, hurts and disappointments but do not know how best to deal with these toxic feelings. They bottle them up inside but since this is not the real solution to these challenges, they soon begin to let out their frustrations by being cranky and irritable. If the condition persists, they can slip into depression and begin to manifest symptoms of bipolar disorder. Naturally, their relationship with others is often negatively affected.

Why am I telling you this? It is to let you see the power of emotional intelligence and why you need to develop it. When you see some people, who will not greet or mind other people, it may not be that they are proud or snobbish; it may just be that they have a mood-related issue at that point. Without taking time to understand them, you may jump to a wrong conclusion and even complicate their plight. So, rather than adding to anyone's burden, ensure to understand them and let them be; or, better still, help them find a way around their mood with kind smiles and related gestures which may awaken the good side of them.

This reminds me of an experience I had with someone who had this mood swing syndrome. Each time I greeted him, he seemed to get offended and sometimes responded with a turned-up nose. I must admit that, at a point, I was tempted to ignore him off and act like he just did not exist to me; but I chose to fight for him, for us. I gradually studied his emotions and began to build a relationship. I continued to show him I cared by greeting him each time we met, adding smiles, and complimenting everything he did. And gradually, the result began to show, and he was able to cast off the cloak of gloominess and unfriendliness.

People often describe mood swings as a "roller coaster" of feelings, from happiness and contentment to anger, irritability, and even depression. A smart person may recognize something that has "triggered" a shift in their mood, such as a stressful event at work, but it is also not uncommon for mood swings to occur without an obvious cause. People may experience these changes in mood over the course of a day or even within a couple of hours and that could affect the way they relate with others. This is why you may be ignored when you greet or try to be nice to them.

Your grumpy co-worker might, for example, say, they "woke up on the wrong side of the bed" when they arrive at the office. They may be feeling so irritable that they would not want to be friendly and may not even greet those that are supposed to be their best pals. This behavior may appear insulting to you while you are simply trying to greet and know how they have been. When you see them later in the day, their mood may have improved. In fact, they may not even recall why they were in a bad mood before.

Let me emphasize here that I am not in any way supporting or defending people who allow their moods to get the better part of them. As I earlier mentioned, we need emotional intelligence – first for ourselves and secondly for others. When we transfer our pains, hurts and concerns to the outside world through bad moods and actions, it portrays us as being self-centered, inconsiderate, and disrespectful. Therefore, it is important to have a good grasp of our emotions at every point in time.

Be the Difference
It is important to know how to handle emotions when it comes to relating with people who may not be nice to you. As you continue to do the right thing, no matter what the other person has portrayed, it gives you the advantage to help them change to a better version of themselves, as well as taking them away from the hangover of pain and whatever may have caused their sullen mood.

The ability to monitor your own and other

people's emotions is key to accurately identifying between different emotions. This will help you to better understand people and to know what action to take at every point in time. In other words, emotional intelligence and awareness will guide your thinking and behavior, such that you are able to approach or address every emotion with the right response.

Generally, emotional intelligence encompasses the following abilities:

Perceiving emotions – This is the ability to detect and decipher emotions in another person, to make accurate discoveries of their mood and temperament using subjective experience by interpreting their physical changes through sensory systems responsible for converting these perceptions. Perception is acquiring knowledge of another person's emotions through words, facial expression, pictures, and cultural artifacts, and almost every way a person shows off his emotions, including the ability to identify one's own emotions. Perceiving emotions represents a basic aspect of emotional intelligence, as it makes all other processing of emotional information possible.

Washington dictates that to accurately perceive emotions, to know how someone is feeling, it is almost better to close your eyes and use your ears, people tend to read others and understand what their mood is by listening and not looking. When you are able to perceive someone's negative mood and position at a period in time, it will be wise to adjust to the person's position and allow wisdom lead you to how to relate with such a person.

Using emotions – in relating with people of different mood and character, you can use emotion to gain their trust and response to you. This is the ability to create attraction and bridge gaps that comes with misunderstanding. Emotions are powerful tools to make the other person listen to you and change their intended negative response or intended approach which may have been built up by pressure or pain. To facilitate various cognitive activities, such as thinking and problem-solving. The emotionally intelligent person can change the way other people respond to them, they greet with passion that nobody will want to ignore them. This is seen with those managing people with disabilities or bipolar disorder, they use emotions to keep a highly upset person to calmness and create trust in them.

To using emotions to build relationships, especially those relationships that relates with those we find so difficult to deal with, we respond by silence or act of care and listening instead of applying force, the emotionally intelligent person knows how to stay calm during stressful situations, they don't make impulsive decisions, that can lead to bigger problem for the person or themselves, but rather understand that in times of conflict, the goal is a resolution, and a conscious choice to focus on ensuring that their actions and words are in alignment with that.

Understanding emotions –This reflects the ability to comprehend emotional language, understand moods and knowing when and how to handle people with such situation. It is also to appreciate complicated relationships which is as a result of some sort of misunderstanding and misbehavior among emotions. For example, understanding emotions encompasses the ability to be sensitive to know a difficult or arrogant person and how their behavior can affect those around them. They also pick up on other people's emotions and body language and use that information to enhance their communication skill with them. When you can understand the mood and action of a stressed person, you are likely to change them quickly and easily from negative to positive.

Getting to understand a person's mood if there is pending provocation affecting the person's attitude towards others is a halfway to solving it. A person's attitude towards others can determine how they will feel and act throughout the day and if they will respond to you positively, a negative attitude easily infects others if it is allowed to continue, emotional intelligent people have a skill of knowing the mood of those around them and guard their attitude effectively. Emotional intelligent people are self-aware and intuitive, they are aware of their own emotion and they are able to adjust when they are about to be rude with others, they begin to smile and give off a positive presence, they utilize appropriate social skills based on their relationship with whomever they are around. They have great interpersonal skills and know how to communicate clearly, whether the communication is verbal or nonverbal.

Managing emotions – This involves the ability to regulate emotions in both ourselves and in others. Therefore, the emotionally intelligent person can harness emotions, even negative ones, and manage them to achieve intended goals. The communication between your emotional and rational "brain" is the physical source of emotional intelligence. The pathway for emotional intelligence starts in the brain, at the spinal cord. Your primary senses enter here and must travel to the front of your brain before you can think rationally about your experience with people. However, first they travel through the limbic system, the place where emotions are generated. You don't react right away as project their action. Reacting immediately to emotional triggers can cause more damage and misunderstanding. So, we have an emotional reaction to events before our rational mind get engaged. As you begin to realize, accept, and successfully control your feelings about others and yourself. Emotional intelligence requires effective communication between the rational and emotional centers of the brain, and this helps to increase our understanding of the reasons for people's actions.

5
NONVERBAL GREETINGS
"Our nonverbal behavior (including posture)
gives away our inner personality and reflects
our inner attitude."
— Cindy Ann Peterson

Nonverbal greetings, which are an aspect of nonverbal communication, may refer to gestures, facial expressions, tone of voice, eye contact, body language, posture, and other ways people can greet without using language. People's words may not be able to reveal the truth about their intentions, but their actions cannot be hidden.

Someone can hide how they feel or the situation they are with words, but his or her facial expression showing disapproval cannot be hidden. Someone who is totally stressed out after waiting long hours for a meeting could tell the secretary who approaches him to ask about his wellbeing that he is totally fine; but by his pulling the collar of his shirt to get some air or by using the back of his hands to wipe his forehead with a sigh, he would definitely tell loads of truth about how he truly feels. Therefore, it is said that "action speaks louder than words."

Your nonverbal gestures when you greet with your actions can say much more than your words. They, in fact, reveal the genuineness or otherwise of your verbal greetings. You may, for instance, say "Hello" to someone but your posture can depict that you would prefer not to greet or have anything to do with the person.

When you show you do not care, chances are that others will not care either; but when you start smiling, others will start smiling with you. No matter the mood they might have been in, once you start being friendly with your gestures, people will become your friends. And when you show humility to others, not minding who is involved, you will influence people to bow their hearts to you.

I have been in situations where I have to greet my harsh and mischievous boss with an upset emotion, I ordinarily will not want to have anything to do with him just after a randy and abusive engagement with me, but he is my boss and I have no choice but to greet and acknowledge his presence. He walked up to me at a particular time and said I should rather not greet him with so much hate and be quiet when he comes in. I was surprised he knew my intentions, I thought someone told him my feelings but he got to know from my expression, the way I squeeze my face when I greet could not be hidden, though I never knew it was that obvious to others.

Let us look at some nonverbal expressions that make the difference in our lives as we meet people everywhere.

Facial Expressions

This way of expression constitutes a huge proportion of nonverbal greetings and communication. Consider how much information can be conveyed with a smile or a frown. The look on a person's face is often the first thing we see, even before we hear what they have to say.

While nonverbal communication and behavior can vary dramatically between cultures, the facial expressions for happiness, sadness, anger, and fear are similar throughout the world. It is important to establish eye contact when speaking to others or greeting them. This will make the receiver of our greeting to know that it is meant for them and that it is sincere.

Use your facial expressions to convey your emotions. Think for a moment about how much a person can convey with just a facial expression. A smile can indicate approval or happiness, a frown can signal disapproval or unhappiness. In some cases, our facial expressions may reveal our true feelings about a situation. You may say that you are feeling fine or approve of someone's presence, but the look on your face may tell people otherwise.

The eyes play an important role in nonverbal communication and such gestures as looking, staring, and blinking are important nonverbal behaviors. When people encounter people or things that they like, the rate of blinking increases and pupils dilate. Looking at another person can indicate a range of emotions including hostility, interest, and attraction.

People also utilize eye gaze to determine if someone is being honest. Normal, steady eye contact is often taken as a sign that a person is telling the truth and is trustworthy. Shifty eyes and an inability to maintain eye contact, on the other hand, is frequently seen as an indicator that someone is lying or being deceptive.

The eyes are frequently referred to as the "windows to the soul" since they can reveal a great deal about what a person is feeling or thinking. As you engage in conversation with another person, taking note of eye movements is a natural and important part of the communication process. Some common things you may notice include whether people are making direct eye contact or averting their gaze, how much they are blinking, or if their pupils are dilated.

When evaluating facial expression, pay attention to the following eye signals:

Eye gaze: When a person looks directly into

your eyes while having a conversation, it indicates that they are interested and paying attention. However, prolonged eye contact can feel threatening. On the other hand, breaking eye contact and frequently looking away might indicate that the person is distracted, uncomfortable, or trying to conceal his or her real feelings.

Blinking: Blinking is natural, but you should also pay attention to whether a person is blinking too much or too little. People often blink more rapidly when they are feeling distressed or uncomfortable. Infrequent blinking may indicate that a person is intentionally trying to control his or her eye movements.[7] For example, a poker player might blink less frequently because he is purposely trying to appear unexcited about the hand he was dealt.

Pupil size: Pupil size can be a very subtle nonverbal communication signal. While light levels in the environment control pupil dilation, sometimes emotions can also cause small changes in pupil size. For example, you may have heard the phrase "bedroom eyes" used to describe the look someone gives when they are attracted to another person. Highly dilated eyes, for example, can indicate that a person is interested or even aroused

Gestures

Deliberate movements and signals are an important way to communicate meaning without words. Common gestures include waving, pointing, and using fingers to indicate numeric amounts. In courtroom settings, lawyers have been known to utilize different nonverbal signals to attempt to sway juror opinions. An attorney might glance at his watch to suggest that the opposing lawyer's argument is tedious or might even roll his eyes at the testimony offered by a witness to undermine his or her credibility. These nonverbal signals are being so powerful and influential that some judges even place limits on what type of nonverbal behaviors are allowed in the courtroom.

In relating with people, we show good manners by making acceptable and appealing gestures. By so doing, we make our bodies to align with the goodness we have built on our inside.

Gestures, when properly used at home, between spouses or between parents and children can help create togetherness and strengthen family bond. Without words, the children can hear their parents talk to them; they understand their body language, and this helps them when relating with outsiders.

Gestures can be some of the most direct and obvious body language signals. Some gestures may be cultural, however, so giving a thumbs-up or a peace sign in another country might have a completely different meaning than it does in the another.

The following examples are just a few common gestures and their possible meanings:

A clenched fist can indicate anger in some situations or solidarity in others. This could mean that someone is unwilling to embrace another person's action, making one look like been ready for a fight or attack, a show of anger.

Thumbs up and thumbs down are often used as gestures of approval and disapproval.

The "okay" gesture made by touching together the thumb and index finger in a circle while extending the other three fingers can be used to mean "okay" or "all right. "In some parts of Europe, however, the same signal is used to imply you are nothing. In some South American countries, the symbol is a vulgar gesture.

The V sign, created by lifting the index and middle finger and separating them to create a V-shape, means peace or victory in some countries. In the United Kingdom and Australia, the symbol takes on an offensive meaning when the back of the hand is facing outward

Body Language and Posture

Posture and movement can also convey a great deal of information. Research on body language has grown significantly since the 1970s, but popular media have focused on the over-interpretation of defensive postures, arm-crossing, and leg-crossing, especially after publishing Julius Fast's book *Body Language*. While these nonverbal behaviors can indicate feelings and attitudes, research suggests that body language is far more subtle and less definitive than previously believed.

How we hold our bodies can also serve as an important part of body language. The term *posture* refers to how we hold our bodies as well as the overall physical form of an individual. Posture can convey a wealth of information about how a person is feeling as well as hints about personality characteristics, such as whether a person is confident, open, or submissive.

Sitting up straight, for example, may indicate that a person is focused and paying attention to what is going on. Sitting with the body hunched forward, on the other hand, can imply that the person is bored or indifferent.

When you are trying to read body language, try to notice some of the signals that a person's posture can send.

- **Open posture** involves keeping the trunk of the body open and exposed. This type of posture indicates friendliness, openness, and willingness.

- **Closed posture** involves hiding the trunk of the body often by hunching forward and keeping the arms and legs crossed. This type of posture can be an indicator of hostility, unfriendliness, and anxiety.

Proxemics (Personal space)

People often refer to their need for "personal space," which is also an important type of nonverbal communication. The amount of distance we need and the amount of space we perceive as belonging to us is influenced by a number of factors, including social norms, cultural expectations, situational factors, personality characteristics, and level of familiarity.

For example, the amount of personal space needed when having a casual conversation with another person usually varies between 18 inches to four feet. On the other hand, the personal distance needed when speaking to a crowd of people is around 10 to 12 feet.

Have you ever heard someone refer to their need for personal space? Have you ever started to feel uncomfortable when someone stands just a little too close to you?

The term *proxemics*, coined by anthropologist Edward T. Hall, refers to the distance between people as they interact. Just as body movements and facial expressions can communicate a great deal of nonverbal information, so can this physical space between individuals.

Hall described the four level of social distance that occur in different situations:

- **Intimate distance— 6 to 18 inches:** This level of physical distance often indicates a closer relationship or greater comfort between individuals. It usually occurs during intimate contact such as hugging, whispering, or touching.

- **Personal distance— 1.5 to 4 feet:** Physical distance at this level usually occurs between people who are family members or close friends. The closer the people can comfortably stand while interacting can be an indicator of the level of intimacy in their relationship.

- **Social distance— 4 to 12 feet:** This level of physical distance is often used with individuals who are acquaintances. With someone you know well, such as a co-worker you see several times a week, you might feel more comfortable interacting at a closer distance. In cases where you do not know the other person well, such as a postal delivery driver you only see once a month, a distance of 10 to 12 feet may feel more comfortable.

- **Public distance— 12 to 25 feet:** Physical distance at this level is often used in public speaking situations. Talking in front of a class full of students or giving a presentation at work are good examples of such situations.

It is also important to note that the level of personal distance that individuals need to feel comfortable can vary from culture to culture. One oft-cited example is the difference between people from Latin cultures and those from North America. People from Latin countries tend to feel more comfortable standing closer to one another as they interact, while those from North America need more personal distance.

Paralinguistic

Paralinguistic refer to aspects of vocal communication that do not involve words. These elements include tone of voice, loudness, inflection, and pitch. Consider the powerful effect that tone of voice can have on the meaning of an expression. When something is said with a strong tone of voice, listeners might interpret approval and enthusiasm. The same words said in a hesitant tone of voice might convey disapproval and a lack of interest.

Consider all the different ways that simply changing your tone of voice might change the meaning of a sentence. A friend might ask you how you are doing, and you might respond with the standard "I'm fine," but how you actually say those words might reveal a tremendous amount of how you are really feeling.

A cold tone of voice might suggest that you are not fine, but you do not wish to discuss it. A bright, happy tone of voice will reveal that you are doing quite well. A somber, downcast tone would indicate that you are the opposite of fine and that perhaps your friend should inquire further.

Mouth expressions and movements can also be essential in reading body language. For example, chewing on the bottom lip may indicate that the individual is experiencing feelings of worry, fear, or insecurity.

Covering the mouth may be an effort to be polite if the person is yawning or coughing, but it may also be an attempt to cover up a frown of disapproval. Smiling is perhaps one of the greatest body language signals, but smiles can also be interpreted in many ways. A smile may be genuine, or it may be used to express false happiness, sarcasm, or even cynicism.

When evaluating paralinguistic, pay attention to the following mouth and lip signals:

Pursed lips: Tightening the lips might be an indicator of distaste, disapproval, or distrust.

Lip biting: People sometimes bite their lips

when they are worried, anxious, or stressed.

Covering the mouth: When people want to hide an emotional reaction, they might cover their mouths to avoid displaying smiles or smirks.

Turned up or down: Slight changes in the mouth can also be subtle indicators of what a person is feeling. When the mouth is slightly turned up, it might mean that the person is feeling happy or optimistic. On the other hand, a slightly down-turned mouth can be an indicator of sadness, disapproval, or even an outright grimace.

Haptics

Communicating through touch is another important nonverbal behavior. You can greet with a simple touch to the shoulder, hands, and wrist. There has been a substantial amount of research on the importance of touch when relating with people or trying to greet with much intimacy and passion.

Harry Harlow's classic study on monkeys demonstrated how deprivation in touch and physical contact impedes development in the animals. Baby monkeys raised by wire mothers (wire effigy of a "mom," complete with a nipple and bottle) experienced permanent deficits in behavior and social interaction.

Touch can be used to communicate affection, familiarity, sympathy, and other emotions. In her book, Interpersonal Communication: Everyday Encounters, author Julia Wood writes that touch is also often used to communicate both status and power. Researchers have found that high-status individuals tend to invade other people's personal space with greater frequency and intensity than lower-status individuals.

Sex differences also play a role in how people utilize touch to communicate meaning. Women tend to use touch to convey care, concern, and nurturance. Men, on the other hand, are more likely to use touch to assert power or control over others.

Appearances

Our choice of color, clothing, hairstyles, and other factors affecting appearance are also considered a means of nonverbal communication.

Research on color psychology has demonstrated that different colors can evoke different moods. Appearance can also alter physiological reactions, judgments, and interpretations.

Just think of all the subtle judgments you quickly make about someone based on his or her appearance. These first impressions are important, which is why experts suggest that job seekers dress appropriately for interviews with potential employers.

Researchers have found that appearance can play a role in how people are perceived and even how much they earn. One 1996 study found that attorneys who were rated as more attractive than their peers earned nearly 15 percent more than those ranked as less attractive.

Culture is an important influence on how appearances are judged. While thinness tends to be valued in Western cultures, some African cultures relate full-figured bodies to better health, wealth, and social status.

Artifacts

Objects and images are also tools that can be used to communicate nonverbally. On an online forum, for example, you might select an avatar to represent your identity online and to communicate information about who you are and the things you like. People often spend a great deal of time developing an image and surrounding themselves with objects designed to convey information about the things that are important to them.

Uniforms, for example, can be used to transmit a tremendous amount of information about a person. A soldier will prefer camouflage, a police officer will wear a uniform, and a doctor will wear a white lab coat. At a mere glance, these outfits tell people what a person does for a living.

6
WE ALL CAN CHANGE

"To change a habit, make a conscious decision, then act out the new behavior."
-Maxwell Maltz

Every day presents us with an opportunity to learn something new, and thus progressively become a better version of ourselves. Regardless of how we may have fared in the past in our interpersonal relationships, I believe that application of the amazing principles we have discovered in our exploration of this all-important subject of greeting will beautifully transform our interactions with others, as well as the image we project to all who come in contact with us.

However, for there to be a transformation or improvement, we must first accept the need to change and then consciously apply the necessary steps to actualize this. Leo Buscalgia aptly said, "Knowing that one is always capable of change, the second step lies in making the decision to change. Change does not occur by merely willing it any more than behavior changes simply through insight."

Therefore, with regard to improving our manners, the first truth we must accept and apply is that we can add tangible value to people's lives and establish mutually beneficial relationships through our decision to greet them, and to do it properly. Hitherto, it may have been hard for you to relate with people, generally, or perhaps with certain people; and you may have even lost potential friends in the process. It is also possible that you have made a few enemies because you had always thought you were the one deserving more of respect because of your status, position, or privileges in life. I can assure you that your negative experiences can be changed. You can win; you can change things for the better. You can make your home beautiful again and win people to your side. You can metamorphose!

Change Begins with You

Most of us long to be recognized, respected, and adored; but we often get it all wrong by demanding for these expectations, rather than attracting them, we claim that since we are the superior or the head of the home, others ought to respect us unreservedly. What we forget however is that respect is reciprocal, and it begins from the leader and the more mature mind.

Ordinarily, it would appear that the one who greets and shows respect is the lesser or subordinate person but that is untrue. In fact, in true leadership, when you show respect and give attention to people, they will by all means subject themselves to your supremacy and surrender to the power of your love -no matter their state of mind or whatever agenda is hidden within their hearts.

A loving and humble heart is always sensitive to the feelings of others. Sadly, not everyone possesses this because it is not inborn; it must be developed. If you study the lives of tremendously successful people, those who have made great impacts in their communities and the world at large, you will find out that they are often humble and friendly. They respect people genuinely, and their manners will begin to depict that they are different, they are rich inside and out, with reverence.

True wealth makes you humble and kind. You will always find yourself happy because the people around you are happy, and you made them happy. Indeed, to be successful and still have peace of mind, you must consciously cultivate some attitudes and habits – which include respecting other people, being humble and being kind. Lack of feeling or respect for others is a clear sign of weakness and a diminutive mind.

Steps to Change

If you have been having problems in your relationship with others, you can consider learning some simple tricks that will turn the tide in your favor.

First is to see everybody as important and respect them as you would want them to respect you. In addition, you can learn to put on a smile as always as possible. This is a natural charm for attraction; no one looks away or get offended by a face that is wearing a smile. Also, learn to make yourself approachable. Do not give people the impression that you are a strong face or a far superior person that is too privileged or principled to be approached.

Moreover, it will help if you do not get easily repelled by people's temporary moodiness. Irrespective of how someone may appear, just go ahead, and show some love. Your love, respect and good manners can change anyone's mood for the better. Your respectful attitude will infiltrate their heart and make them be at peace with you.

Your sincere respect for others is what makes you stay ahead of them. People think that the lesser should show respect and greet the better or greater, but that is not true of life's dynamics. Your greeting does not just show respect, it commands it! If you are humble enough to give respect and value to others, you show how mature you are and why you should always be at the forefront of leadership.

Give others respect, no matter their age, race,

or face. Do not let your status or position get in the way. As a matter of fact, trying to be choosy or discriminatory in showing respect is a faulty attitude that comes with unnecessary headache. Suppose you are the boss in an organization with people always waiting in a queue to adore you like a demigod, will you radiate sensitivity and show respect? at least, reciprocate. Maybe you are in the house with your spouse and a misunderstanding ensued, then you begin to wonder who is supposed to break the unnerving silence and be the first to greet, because you think apologizing or making peace with your spouse is an act of cowardice. Yet the real strong or successful person is the peacemaker who knows how to keep a relationship and win respect.

True humility is characterized by how you can swallow your pride and ignore offenses. It puts you in the position to create the atmosphere and determine the mood you want to see in the people you love. This way, you gain their attention and respect.

Apparently, acceptability and relationship are interwoven. For you to build a lasting and meaningful relationship, you must learn self-control and forgiveness, coupled with intentional affection. This will help you to win the trust and respect of your spouse and everyone else.

A Rottweiler's Sermon

Bruddy, my neighbor's dog is an amazing Rottweiler, with the qualities of a Havanese dog - big, bold, and almost too friendly to be a Rottweiler. It is a dog I like so much. Something interesting happened with this dog that I considered quite instructive, that makes me want to share it. At a time, Mr. Alex, its owner, traveled and left the Dog with his cousin, Bryan, who unfortunately is not a lover of dogs. Soon after Mr. Alex's departure, Bryan began to treat Bruddy with so much cruelty, as if he were waiting for such opportunity to come. He would often beat the Dog with his belt, tie it to a pole and starve it all day.

I felt deep pain and compassion for Bruddy daily, as I watched its suffering from my balcony or through the fence. There were days I was forced often time with compassion to take food out of my fridge to serve the dog. Ironically, however, the dog seemed to be in love with Bryan still, such that, whenever he returned, this Dog would vigorously wag its tail in excitement. It would try to stand up with its back legs holding up the whole body. Its fur would rise and stand erect like a hairdresser's brush.

I could not stop to wonder how stupid this dog was. It clearly had the opportunity to fight back whenever Bryan brought out his belt to whip it. Or could just ignore him whenever he returned from work to express displeasure of his dastardly acts, but anytime it heard the sound of Bryan's old Nissan Sentra car driving into the garage, the dog would start running towards him with warmth and joy, barking loud.

I watched these happenings from day to day. That it happened again, and this time I decided I was going to put a stop to Bryan's brutality against this innocent Rottweiler. I decided to confront the heavily bearded 21-year-old man, but to my surprise, he had brought out a bag full of assorted food, meat, and other treats for Bruddy. They seemed to have suddenly become friends, as the Dog rushed to him, they jumped on each other like a newly found missing old friend. Well, since I was in the compound already, I still decided to have a chat with Bryan.

Bruddy the Dog did not for once give up its honor and loyalty to its new master, despite Bryan's attitude. And of course, its forbearance and patience seemed to have finally melted Bryan's heart and won him over. Bryan's attitude changed towards the dog in the course of time. But this only happened because Bruddy never gave up being true to its love and respect and that created a different relationship with them.

This same approach can be applied in our daily life. People may be unkind to us or sometimes rebuff our kindness to them, but we must not stop being good mannered; we must continue greeting and showing the much respect and love because we carry the power of change within us.

I know there are still some folks who wonder why they should seek peace, even when they are the ones offended or when they are not getting a good response from the other person they are greeting. This situation has caused so many broken homes, husbands and wives getting terribly upset with each other with accusation of pride. Well, it is time to change things by cultivating a different habit which will help you live well and amicably with others and your loved ones.

You must begin to tell yourself that it is your responsibility to show care, love, and attention to others because that is all you need to become even more successful and fulfilled. You should start changing from the negative side of pride and ignorance. You must train your mind to remind you that the people you meet all the time deserve your respect and that you will begin to show it by greeting them with a respectful smile.

Should You Greet First?

This is an issue for some people; yet it really should not be. Greeting someone you know is a vital part of courtesy and goodwill, and a proof that you are a respectable personality. All societies have some form of greeting. They are basic to civilized interactions.

The first point about greetings is to *do them*. It is important to say "Hello" even when you feel a bit cranky or shy. It is also important to make introductions even when you are not certain of precisely how it should be done in that situation. Every greeting and introduction are an opportunity to demonstrate respect for others and to create a favorable impression of yourself to others.

When you greet someone, you acknowledge their presence and you announce your presence too. Most people do this automatically and barely notice they are doing it; they have been so cultured to be polite, heartwarming and kind. But failing to offer a greeting to someone you know can easily cause hurt to their feelings and misunderstandings – you are failing to acknowledge their existence in your presence. Little can be considered more offensive than deliberately ignoring someone, as this strikes to the heart of the most basic of human needs, inclusion, and social interaction.

If someone who usually greet others in a friendly way does not, people may feel snubbed or think the person is behaving oddly or carrying an unsettled offense. This can happen for a variety of reasons, such as being preoccupied or distracted, being late for an appointment and rushing, or even forgetting their glasses and not being able to recognize someone they know. Usually these omissions can be corrected with a warm greeting to the person, it is a way to draw the person's attention to his error or misconduct. This character illustrates the first essentials of manner, which is greeting, and which is where people start their judgement about who you are.

If you know the person, whether a neighbor, co-worker, or acquaintance, both of you should greet each other in some way without thought. Love is not biased; it does not see wrongs or count another person's misbehavior. In fact, there is no charm equal to tenderness of heart. You aggressively make things work and make people learn what humanity is all about.

Maturity is when you do not hold to the heart what the other person has done wrong; rather, you are busy with making everything right and keeping friendship. Maturity does not mean age, it means sensitivity, and does not enforce who is to greet who first as a mark of seniority, an elder can greet a younger at any point in time, this is a sign of love and not cowardice, and it is a transfer of knowledge of what a good example should look like from a mature mind to the upcoming ones. It projects good manners and how to react in any situation. Many people out there have politeness problem though. They were either not taught manners, or they do not remember how it is used.

It should not be a contest to be courteous. If you have always been initiating the greeting, that is not a bad thing to do, it means you are getting even better and more mature in mind; you are getting to climb the ladder of success quickly. It opens your mind to understanding more of kindness and respect for others, irrespective of their age or culture. If you have been in the habit of greeting and respecting people naturally, you will not notice or remember if you have been the one greeting first or the other person.

That said, let me point this out quickly, that it

is impolite to enter an occupied space without greeting those who are already there. If you do not greet, then you are rude; you are noticed as not being a friend and will lose the first level of control.

I know how annoying this can be when there is a discomfort forced upon you because someone else is not being polite or even respectful, but it should not be an issue for you if you already have manners. You just make every moment fun and make everybody see things differently. Your greeting to someone who may not regard your gesture does not undermine your personality rating; rather it gives you an advantage over them.

I will not think twice about greeting someone who failed to follow proper etiquette. I believe that as I do the right thing, I immediately teach them good manners and open myself to greater respect. Shyness is some people's problem, while some others simply lack training to do the right thing, and for some, it is arrogance.

Sometimes, you may not be sure that you have recognized the correct individual to greet but you can always say "hello" first. There is no rule or law in this world that says you should not greet first or choose who to greet and not to greet; I do not bother wondering if someone is being aloof or perhaps arrogant. I do not care, nor do I think it matters. I say "hello" first because it is friendly, it is fun, it is happiness, it is peaceful, and it will always be to my advantage in the long run. It makes me feel confident and in control, and because I would rarely get to speak with someone with whom I am unacquainted if I did not do so.

You may be waiting for me to advise that you ignore anyone you greeted more times without an answer and will always feel pompous and always waiting and expecting you to greet each time. That could have been a solution to the rudeness of some people, but that does not correct the person or the situation, rather, as you continue to do the right thing and been an example of good manners, that person will begin to change and do the right thing as expected.

Saying "hello" first makes me feel empowered; it is an assurance that whenever I ask, I will get an answer in return because I have opened myself to favor and gotten a space in the person's heart.

Reaping the Rewards

As has been earlier emphasized, choosing to improve in our manners and relationship with others, even when it is not convenient, comes with huge benefits and I can personally testify to this. I was once a marketing executive with MFI & Associates INC, in the days when yellow pages were still the best business directory and way to get company information and data. The company had mandated that every salesperson should sell at least 30 pieces of the yellow pages per day. I knew, from the very first day, that I will not meet up with that target because I had never really been a good marketer. I was always a shy person, could not talk much and, worse still, dreaded the shame of rejection.

Well, as should be expected, I did not do well with the targets and my initial excuse was that I had never done any sort of selling before. Still, I did not give up. There was this prospective client on Broad Street, a rubber manufacturing company that had grown into a flagship company. I had always wished they would place an advert on the front page of the directory and buy as much copies for the marketing staff to use for business, as that would be my big break. Getting companies to place adverts in the directory was where the money was, and I knew that alone would make up for my failure in the daily target.

I decided to give it a shot. I requested for the company's details from my cousin, who was once a staff with them, he gave me as much information as I needed. He also advised me on how I was going to reach and talk to the secretary about my mission and how I was going to get an appointment with the procurement manager or the CEO. Looking forward to this plan, I headed for the company on the morning of the following Monday and got there too early. Only a few of the company staff had resumed for the day's work. I was not bothered about that as I sat in the reception facing the office of the secretary to the CEO. I cheerfully greeted the people I met and thereafter spent some time looking around and studying the paintings on the wall.

Soon, more people started coming in and, despite my anxiety, I kept smiling and greeting them as they entered. I never bothered to know who worked there or who was just a visitor, I never also bothered about who I met or who met me in the reception, I greeted everyone who was there with me. In fact, I tried keeping everyone in high spirit.

After some time, I noticed a bald head man come into the reception, looking angry and restless. He kept staring at his phone, as if he were expecting an important call. He was well dressed, looking sharp and neat, but I was almost started disliking him, because he seemed arrogant and domineering. I greeted him as he sat close to me, but he never responded, though he looked at me and saw the big smile on my face. I concluded that he was probably too tense as he came for the same purpose as mine. This made me to say, "Hello" to him again. This time around, he looked straight into my eyes and fixed his gaze on me briefly and eventually seemed to look away with a scorn. Undaunted, I told him he looked good and sharp and encouraged him to expect something great out of his visit. This made him to look at me again, this time with a grin. He was probably surprised that I could greet and wish him well, again and again, despite his rudeness. Then, I added, still smiling, "Meeting people for the first time can be tough, but with confidence and a positive mind, you will always succeed." Almost immediately, he got up, walked into where I thought was the secretary's office and never came out.

By the next hour, the office was full and bustling with activities - people walking in and out carrying files and other office materials. My anxiety returned in full force when the secretary approached me and asked me if I had an appointment. I told her I would like to see the CEO or any other senior officer of the company as I have an important business to discuss with. As we kept talking, I noticed someone pointing at me from the glass door, facing where I was. I soon discovered that it was the bald man and he is the CEO I was looking for. At this time, the secretary was almost asking me to leave as I have overstayed my welcome in the office and never even had a previous appointment. But just then the CEO called me into his office and asked me what he could do for me. This was an open cheque, and it was indeed a groundbreaking success, I never imagined I could get to success so quickly and easily, just from been unrepentantly good and nice, and following good greeting etiquette.

Soon after, the company had a meeting with me and gave me an appointment to submit and defend my proposal. Eventually, I got the contract and the process turned out a huge success! Indeed, good manners pay a lot – if we can first make the sacrifice!

7
CHARACTER TRAITS FOR RELATIONSHIP MASTERY

"As a man's salutations, so is the total of his character; in nothing do we lay ourselves so open as in our manner of meeting and salutation.

Johann Caspar Lavater

It has been an interesting, enlightening, and enriching journey so far, and I am certain that many life-changing lessons have been learned along the way. We have established that our greetings and the way we do them, are the windows to our character. We have seen, with relevant examples and illustrations, that good manners are indispensable in helping to make a good first impression, establish good relationships, gain people's confidence, and set a positive tone for any conversation, whether it is with a friend, a boss or a client.

As we wrap up these wonderful expositions, here are the key character traits you will need to be able to put all you have learned so far into good use and get the desired results:

Be open to new people and ideas
One of the most important traits you will find in a person with good manners is to greet and speak to others from various backgrounds and cultures with respect and openness. This means he must be culturally sensitive, which is a quality that comes naturally to those who score high on being open to new things. Being open-minded helps to creatively solve problems and ensure that every person you meet is attended to in a respectful and polite manner.

Learn to control your emotions
It is quite common for well-cultured people to find themselves in a fix as they meet different kinds of people. When someone corners you with a negative attitude, it is hard not to feel threatened or become emotionally defensive. But it is critical to remain calm, so that you can prevail with your loving and caring attitude. Eventually, you will find that people will accord

you a different level of respect and attention, and friendship will continue to run smoothly.

Even when someone is being difficult or even aggressive in their tone, you must strive to remain absolute in your position. Remember, you must stay true to your real self. So, staying strong in your stance is a must. Add this in mind that, Love is the only force that can turn an enemy to a friend, and it starts from your approach towards people. Your attitude when you are detested and when you are not supposed to be nice and greeting even at the odd periods when you have all the right to be at the offensive, is all that matters.

Be empathetic always
Sometimes you meet with people who are sad, upset, or irate. In fact, people can have varying emotions when they meet you maybe for the first time or over time. Through it all, however, an important quality for a friendly disposition is to be able to sense and recognize these emotions and address them properly. This means you must be empathetic.

If you have found a person who is able to put

themselves in another person's shoes, then you have found a good person with great manners. It is not an easy task for anyone to put themselves aside for another's feelings or wellbeing, but for those that can do this, they make the best candidates for success and other great opportunities.

Maintain your composure, even under pressure

We often work or relate with people under high amounts of stress. There can be some downtime or slower periods in the average day, and you may suddenly find yourself juggling many things at once. There are always deadlines to meet, meetings to schedule, calls to make, and dozens of other things to finish up, none of which can be postponed. Added to these are family responsibilities, personal struggles and so on. Put together, this may cause a lot of strain on you.

Nevertheless, a person with a good personality trait is one that can handle things gracefully, respect others and extend respect to those they meet or come in contact with at every point in time.

Keep your emotions in check

A person with good manners and controlled emotions remains unmoved and able to make rational decisions, even when there is a reason for chaos. If someone is angry with you and almost getting aggressive, find a calm way to make them reason, rather than "returning fire for fire". Do not let things escalate to the point that you are dragged into doing the unthinkable and soiling your good reputation. You must "keep your wits about you" at all times.

Think strategically

When the time comes, and it will, a person with good manners will have to make some big decisions regarding the people they meet. Your ability to tame uncontrollable outbursts and irrational behaviors will be tested often. This is especially common when the other person is not just ready to calm down and allow you act rightly with them. Your ability to control your emotions and make the right decisions to handle the situation will be highly needed at such times.

Be patient

The most important virtue and personality trait of a person with good manners is patience. "Patience is a virtue" - but it is also a personality trait. You can patiently relate with anybody you meet anywhere and at any time. Handling situations calmly and listening to people before speaking are critical here. In fact, without patience, you really cannot be successful in your relationship with people.

Be friendly and polite

Being friendly and polite is a characteristic that comes naturally to some people, but it is also a quality that can be learned. Friendly and polite people always speak with a smile, are kind and resourceful, and ensure that they do not cross the boundaries of civility. Even when you have all the powers and privileges to belittle or snub others, you still must choose the path of honor and humility. The true measure of a person is how they treat those that can do absolutely nothing for them.

Be sociable

Being extroverted can be immensely helpful in dealing with people and meeting their emotional needs. However, this does not mean introverts cannot be sociable. Introverts can be quite sociable, if they find time to empathize more with others, as well as developing enthusiasm to help others in every way possible.

Be judicious and careful

If you are working on your personality and want to be the best you can be in relating with people, make sure you pay good attention to details. One of the most important habits you must develop is to take notes and record information, as much as possible. Notice the kind of people you are relating with. Observation is key, but it does not really have to do with physical looking; rather, it is the communication of the mind. Study the people you are relating with. What are their mannerisms, tendencies, and preferences? Entering and processing the necessary details in your thoughts will make you more prudent and practical in your relationship with everybody, no matter their personality or mood.

156

To sum it all up, having wonderful relationships with people and having a positive impact in their lives require having good manners, especially greeting them properly. Characteristics that will make this easy for you include being open-minded, friendly, sociable, careful, diligent, empathetic, patient, and always being in control of your emotions. It might seem like a tall order, considering the level of irritability and irrationality that you have to put up with daily from others; but possessing the qualities embedded in good manners, as already highlighted, will position you for unlimited accomplishments in your personal life, professional pursuits and family responsibilities.

Epilogue

Hate no one, no matter how much they have wronged you, live humbly, no matter how wealthy you become, think positively, no matter how hard life is, give much, even if you have been given little, forgive all, especially yourself. And never stop praying for the best for everyone.

I always tell those who care to listen that when they live a life without hurt or disregard, then it means they never did anything worthy to get reproached. The beauty of life is what lives inside it, not just the success, joy or the wealth or respect, but the disappointments, offenses, pains and neglect that comes from the people we have relationship with and those we least expect such from, Unfortunately, many spend so much time on the disappointments and offenses that come from people and end up becoming victims of such degradation and circumstances. Rather than taking these experiences to translate to be a stone on a stone which is a way to reaching people and transforming them through love and affection and finding fulfilment.

Remember this one thing that holding unto anger is like drinking poison and expecting the other person to die. Learning to live with people, no matter what they do and how they behave, you will always be happy by your own action and the way you give what you have. The fact that the world is full of annoying naughtiness, ungratefulness and rudeness of people, you will always come across them during the gentle stroll of your life, but the best thing to do is to deal with them with love and maturity, you cannot get everyone to behave well and like you all the time, but you can create the kind of atmosphere you want by doing the right things.

Hatred and intolerance have caused many a lot of problem, but there is every possibility that everybody can be happy and fulfilled, just follow the right part, do the right thing the first time, you will be making yourself happy and lifting those who are depressed and ill-mannered to become a better person again.

I was a victim of maltreatment from an overpowering colleague who happen to trust in her ego as an older employee with the small firm we were working with, it almost cost me my job, I was about to leave just because I could not accept her belief that there is a lesser person that is supposed to greet a higher person or that I am meant to greet because it is the rule that makes the rich and better differentiated from the poor and lesser.

My favorite cousin lost her marriage because of this very small act that others see as fun, she was myopic, she stopped taking to her husband as soon as she got offended, she stopped greeting, stopped showing love to her husband and kept away care for her home. She lost it because she never had good understanding.

This book is an eye opener, no one should lose relationships anymore, the way to the top should become smooth and straight because it is, attitude changes everything, a dark gloomy environment, a shredded friendship, a tall wall setting, greeting is a lifestyle, it is a character trait that can make becoming a success easy and build love and peace over unrepentant opposition.

THE END

OTHER BOOKS BY THE AUTHOR

WEALTH OF RICHES

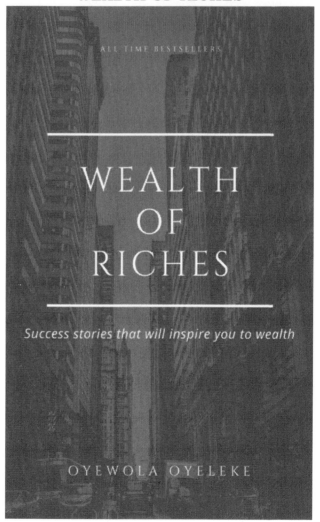

STRONG MEAT

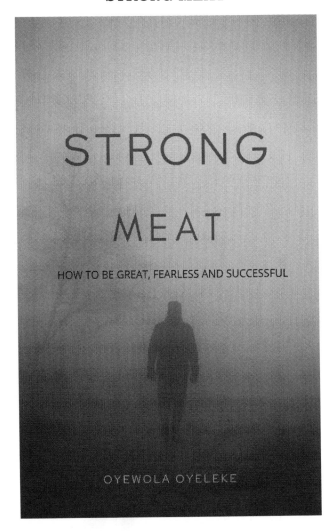

STRONG

MEAT

HOW TO BE GREAT, FEARLESS AND SUCCESSFUL

OYEWOLA OYELEKE